FREE
Indeed

GALATIANS

KEN HEMPHILL
EPILOGUE BY JOHNNY HUNT

Auxano
PRESS

Copyright ©2020 by Ken Hemphill

All Rights Reserved.

ISBN: 978-1-7337059-2-9

Published by Auxano Press, Travelers Rest, South Carolina. www.AuxanoPress.com.

Cover design: CrosslinCreative.net

Cover image: iStock

Unless otherwise noted, Scripture quotations are taken from the New American Standard Bible® (NASB), Copyright © 1960, 1962, 1963, 1968, 1971, 1972, 1973, 1975, 1977, 1995 by The Lockman Foundation. Used by permission. www.Lockman.org.

Scripture quotations marked KJV are from The Authorized (King James) Version. Rights in The Authorized Version in the United Kingdom are vested in the Crown. Used by permission of the Crown's patentee, Cambridge University Press.

Scripture quotations marked NKJV are taken from the New King James Version®. Copyright © 1982 by Thomas Nelson. Used by permission. All rights reserved.

Scripture quotations marked (NIV) are taken from the Holy Bible, New International Version®, NIV®. Copyright © 1973, 1978, 1984, 2011 by Biblica, Inc.™ Used by permission of Zondervan. All rights reserved worldwide. www.zondervan.com. The "NIV" and "New International Version" are trademarks registered in the United States Patent and Trademark Office by Biblica, Inc.™

Printed in the United States of America

24 23 22 21 20—5 4 3 2 1

To
Sam Reece,
our grandson,
whose childlike exuberance for life
brings a smile to our faces.
Our prayer is that your commitment to Christ
will grow daily and
that you will exhibit the fullness
of the fruit of the Spirit.

"It was for freedom that Christ set us free;
therefore keep standing firm
and do not be subject again to a yoke of slavery."
(Gal. 5:1)

Contents

Acknowledgments vii

Introduction ix

Chapter 1 Only One Authentic Gospel
Galatians 1:1-10. 1

Chapter 2 But God!
Galatians 1:11-24. 11

Chapter 3 Entrusted with the Gospel to the Gentiles
Galatians 2:1-10. 21

Chapter 4 The Truth of the Gospel
Galatians 2:11-21. 31

Chapter 5 The Gospel Is Not a Scam
Galatians 3:1-14. 39

Chapter 6 An Irrevocable Covenant
Galatians 3:15-29. 49

Chapter 7 Crying "Abba! Father!"
Galatians 4:1-20 59

Chapter 8 Children of Promise
Galatians 4:21-31. 69

Chapter 9	It Was for Freedom that Christ Set Us Free! **Galatians 5:1-15**. 77	
Chapter 10	The Fruit of the Spirit **Galatians 5:16-24**. 87	
Chapter 11	The Spirit in Community **Galatians 5:25–6:10**. 97	
Chapter 12	Boast in the Cross Alone **Galatians 6:11-18**. 107	

Epilogue 115

Acknowledgments

Every book is a team effort, and persons whose names do not often appear on the cover of the book deserve much of the credit for the finished product. I am grateful to the people at Auxano Press who ensure the accuracy, beauty, and serviceability of the non-disposable curriculum that has become the signature product of this publishing company. I am especially indebted to Maleah Bell, who is the lead editor and project manager at Auxano Press. Her attention to detail and knowledge of the industry ensures the quality of each project. Robin Crosslin designs our covers and interiors, making our products both attractive and readable. Josh Hunt assists greatly in getting materials to Bookmasters in a timely manner. Bookmasters/Baker and Taylor prints, stores, and ships our materials.

I have profited greatly from reading numerous excellent commentaries and books related to the passages considered in this book. Our goal is to keep footnotes to a minimum, and therefore they are used only in the case of a direct citation. I have relied primarily on three key commentaries, which are readily available to the reader: Alan Cole, *Galatians* in Tyndale New Testament Commentaries (London: Tyndale Press, 1971); William Hendriksen, *Exposition of Galatians* in New Testament Commentary series (Grand Rapids, MI: Baker Books, 1968); and Thomas Lea, *Saved by Grace* (Nashville: Convention Press, 1994). To assist those who teach Auxano curriculum, the notes taken from these three sources are available as a free teaching aid from Auxanopress.com.

Paula is my wife, constant companion (during Covid-19), and ministry partner for more than fifty years. She shares my love for God's Word and His world. She manages our home and makes it

Acknowledgments

possible for me to spend hours in my office writing the original drafts for these books.

My children and grandchildren are constantly in mind as I prepare these materials for small group Bible study. My family is the context for my entire writing ministry. The books I write and publish are part of the legacy I am passing on to them. I want them to know God personally and intimately through Jesus. I want them to love and cherish God's Word so they can grow in wisdom, stature, and in favor with God and humanity. A few years ago I began dedicating books to my grandchildren. This is number eleven in the grandkid series, and it is dedicated to Sam Reece.

Tina, our firstborn, far exceeds her dad as an author. Her first book *Given: The Forgotten Meaning and Practice of Blessing* is a life changer. She and her husband Brett have three children—Lois, Micah, and Naomi. Our daughter Rachael exhibits a wonderful gift in helping businesses care for their employees. She and Stephen are proud parents of the "big blend"—Emerson, Ward, Ruby, Audrey, and Sam. Katie, the youngest, is a creative mom who makes every occasion fun. She and Daniel have four children—Aubrey, Sloane, Edie, and Shepherd. Our children and grandchildren bring us great joy and give us great hope for the future of the church.

I want to thank Dr. Gene Fant and all my colleagues at North Greenville University, where "Christ makes the difference." It is my privilege to serve as special assistant to the president for denominational relations and as a distinguished professor. The development of non-disposable small group Bible study material is one facet of North Greenville's strategy to help local churches experience healthy, biblical growth. It is our conviction that only the Word of God applied by the Spirit of God changes the heart and mind.

Introduction

Readers who have used our curriculum, or persons who have heard me preach, know how much I love God's Word. They also know that I am a "bit of a Paulinist." I think many pastors tend to gravitate to the Pauline letters because, after all, they were written to specific churches to deal with real issues that are no different from those faced by the church today. The answers Paul provided as he was guided by the Spirit to pen these occasional letters are of great value to churches today.

I grew up hearing my dad preach from these letters. As I myself began preaching, Paul's letters were my natural starting place. I found them easy to preach from because they virtually outlined themselves. They were, after all, Paul's letters (messages) to his church family. While I attended seminary I used most of my elective hours to study from Paul's writings. As I headed to Cambridge for additional preparation, I chose a dissertation topic about spiritual gifts, which would allow me to focus on two of my great loves, Paul's letters and the local church.

In 2018 I wrote *The Letters of Paul: An Introduction to the Apostle*. I am convinced there is no better way to understand the great missionary than through his personal letters to his churches. As I wrote the Galatians chapter, I realized how essential this letter is for understanding the very essence of the gospel. I am delighted to make it available to local churches for small group study.

Galatians has been called a letter packed with spiritual dynamite. It contains many of the themes in a succinct form that are later fleshed out in Romans. It is of unique significance because it is the first letter written by Paul. Therefore, it is no surprise that Galatians not only provides us with an intimate look at the calling of the apostle, but it also provides an explanation of and a defense of the gospel.

As we read and study the Pauline letters, we need to bear in mind that we are looking at the church in its infancy. These first-century Christians were often caught up in complex crosscurrents, which caused confusion and necessitated further instruction from their founder. In this letter Paul found it necessary to defend his apostolic authority and the gospel he preached. He was intensely concerned that some persons were in danger of deserting the authentic gospel of grace for a distorted view that wanted to add works to grace.

The Larger Context

One of the great lessons I learned from my supervisor and mentor in Cambridge, Professor C.F.D. Moule, was that a person's understanding of any individual letter or text must be based on the larger context of its setting in the life of the church and the author. For that reason we begin with Paul's conversion and subsequent ministry in Antioch.

Paul was a persecutor of Christ who became His proclaimer because of Paul's experience with the risen Jesus on the road to Damascus (Acts 9:1-9). Paul immediately began a powerful preaching ministry, which prompted some Jews to attempt to do away with him (vv. 20-23). He escaped to Jerusalem but was ostracized by many of the disciples who doubted that he was a disciple until Barnabas came to his aid. Paul preached freely in Jerusalem for a period until some Hellenistic Jews rose up against him (vv. 28-29). The brethren sent him to Tarsus, and he ultimately ministered in Arabia for a period (Gal. 1:17).

INTRODUCTION

Paul's church-planting ministry began with the church at Antioch, the church where the gospel was first proclaimed openly to the Gentiles (Acts 11:19-30). Barnabas was sent from Jerusalem to visit the church at Antioch. When he saw what God was doing there, he brought Paul to Antioch to share in the discipling of the new converts. After learning of a global famine, the church sent Paul and Barnabas to Jerusalem with an offering for the relief of the saints (vv. 29-30). This would have occurred around AD 46–47.

When the church at Antioch had gathered for worship, the Spirit instructed the church family to send Paul and Barnabas on a church-planting mission (Acts 13:1-3). Paul and Barnabas went to cities in Asia Minor such as Pisidian Antioch, Iconium, Lystra, and Derbe. Both Jews and Gentiles responded to the gospel, but some Jews strongly opposed Paul's preaching (13:50; 14:1-2, 19).

After Paul completed his missionary journey, he returned to Antioch and spent "a long time" with the disciples (Acts 14:26-28). "Some men" (persons often referred to as Judaizers by many commentators) from Judea came to Antioch teaching that circumcision was necessary for salvation. Paul and Barnabas strongly dissented, and the church sent them to Jerusalem to consult with the apostles and elders on this issue (15:1-2). It is possible that Paul wrote Galatians just prior to the conclusion of the Jerusalem Council (AD 49–50) to deal with the growing controversy concerning what one must do to be saved.

As we study Galatians together, we shall discover that the Judaizers came to Galatia after Paul had established the church. They taught that Gentiles who responded to the Jewish Messiah must also submit to Jewish customs such as circumcision to be saved. Paul knew that such a message distorted the gospel because it added "works" to the simple message of "by grace through faith."

Introduction

To undermine Paul's preaching, his opponents attacked the legitimacy of his apostolic calling (Gal. 1:11–2:10). Paul's defense of his apostolic credentials was, in truth, a defense of the message he preached. The essence of the gospel itself was at stake in Galatia. What must a person do to be a disciple of Christ?

This question and the answer found in the book of Galatians are as relevant today as they were in the first century.

Chapter 1

Only One Authentic Gospel

Galatians 1:1-10

I have been fascinated with coins since childhood. My dad was a pastor in a moderate-sized Baptist church. The offering was usually counted by the deacons soon after the end of the morning worship. I was allowed to go through the change in the offering plate (with adequate adult supervision, I might add) and replace an old coin with a modern one. For example, I would frequently find Indian Head pennies and buffalo nickels, which I would replace with a Jefferson nickel or a wheat penny. I hate to admit that I ultimately spent my precious coins, no doubt for ice cream or a candy bar.

While I was pastoring in Norfolk, a layman stirred my interest in coins once again. This time, at his suggestion, I began buying proof sets from the United States Mint. In time, I began to expand my coin collection by purchasing sets of coins from reputable dealers. I say "reputable" because I was warned that it was possible for a person to purchase a counterfeit coin. It had never occurred to me that someone might want to make a counterfeit copy of a nickel or dime. Yet, considering the value of some collectible coins, you can understand why that might happen.

In writing to the Galatians Paul had to confront the possibility that some members of the church in Galatia were in danger of accepting a "counterfeit" gospel, which, like a counterfeit coin, is worthless. In the case of a counterfeit gospel more was at stake than a mere financial loss; eternity itself hung in the balance. As

CHAPTER 1

we read and study this letter, we will see the apostle's passionate defense of the gospel and his deep-seated love for his fellow believers.

A Reputable Dealer (vv. 1-2)

One way to avoid a counterfeit coin is to buy from a reputable dealer who knows how to spot a counterfeit and is committed to providing only authentic, collectable coins. The best way to avoid a counterfeit gospel is to listen to an authentic apostle whose call and commission has come directly from the risen Christ. As you read Paul's defense of his apostolic credentials, bear in mind that his goal was not to defend himself but to defend the authenticity of the gospel he had been called to preach. This book is about the gospel and not about Paul.

Paul began his letter in the standard letter-writing style of his day. A letter would begin with the name of the sender, followed by that of the recipients and a word of greeting. Often, an amanuensis (personal secretary) would write the bulk of the letter, since letter writing in the first century was a tedious task with writing supplies that were far different from modern-day ink pens and stationery. The author, after dictating the letter, might grab the stylus to add a personal note at the end (6:11).

The name *Paul* was a common Roman surname. Beyond the fact that Paul was a Roman citizen, we know nothing of the origin of his family's citizenship. Paul tells us he was born a Roman citizen (Acts 22:28). It is likely that Paul's birth name, Saul, was used by his family and friends. The apostle may have chosen "Paul" because of its assonance with his Jewish name. After Acts 13:9 Luke consistently referred to the apostle as "Paul." It is entirely likely that Paul used the Roman version of his name for the sake of his Gentile ministry. Such a decision would be consistent with his stated desire to "by all means save some" (1 Cor. 9:22).

The most important identification in the address of this letter is "apostle." When we read the word *apostle*, we most often think of the original twelve disciples. In regular Greek usage an apostle meant a special messenger who enjoyed an authority and commission that came from higher authority than his own. While the word is used in the New Testament in the special sense of the twelve original disciples, it is also used in this broader sense of a special messenger. For example, it is used of James, the brother of Jesus, and a wider and more indefinite group of persons (cf. Rom. 16:7).

Three features distinguish apostles in the more exclusive sense: (1) they had seen the risen Christ (1 Cor. 9:1); (2) they had a personal call from Christ (1 Cor. 1:1); and (3) they had produced spiritual fruit as evidence of this call (1 Cor. 9:2). Paul was not among the Twelve but was qualified to join this group by virtue of his Damascus road experience. First Corinthians 15 speaks of Paul's apostolic authority by indicating he was "untimely born" and a persecutor of the church (vv. 8-9). Even a cursory reading of Paul's letters will demonstrate that his opponents often questioned his claim to be an apostle.

In the introduction of Galatians Paul underlined his apostolic authority, not only to identify himself as an apostle like the Twelve, but also, paradoxically, to set himself off as distinct from that group. Therefore, he began with a denial—his call did not originate from any human authority. The phrase "not sent from men nor through the agency of man" means his call had neither human source nor human agency. Paul linked his call with Jesus the Messiah and the Father who raised Him from the dead. The resurrection is clear proof of Christ's deity and God's power.

Chapter 1

Paul thus demonstrated that his apostolic authority and that of the Twelve must stand or fall together since both rested on the validity of the same historical event. Further, to reject him and his gospel is to reject Christ and the Father who sent Him and raised Him from the dead.

The abrupt opening with its appeal to apostolic authority provides us with clear insight into the purpose of this letter. The Galatians had enthusiastically responded to Paul's preaching (4:14-15). Soon after Paul's departure false teachers had confused the Galatians by suggesting that works of the law were necessary for salvation (3:1-2; 5:12). Paul vigorously opposed these false teachers because the issue was not Paul's reputation but the very essence of the gospel. Salvation comes by grace through faith in Christ alone.

Note that in 1:2 Paul included "the brethren who are with me" as coauthors. Paul wanted the Galatians to know that he did not stand alone in opposition to the Judaizing heresy that had crept into their churches. The word "brethren" had distinguished history in Judaism, but it came to have a richer meaning in the Christian community. Jesus referred to those who heard and obeyed the word of God as His brothers and sisters (Luke 8:21). Thus, in Christ, the "brethren" included all who believed in Christ as Savior and Lord. In this instance "brethren" could refer to (a) Paul's traveling companions; (b) members of the church from which the letter originated; or (c) those in (b) plus a delegation from the Galatian churches.

You may have noticed in Galatians 1:2 that "churches" is plural, indicating that several house churches were in this area and the letter was to be shared with each one. The reference to Paul's signature in 6:11 suggests that Paul sent a single letter that was handed on to each church. It is further possible that each church would have made a copy of the letter. It is important to note that these local churches were in fellowship and cooperation with one another.

Grace and Peace (vv. 3-5)

Although the opening greeting was thoroughly Jewish, in verses 3-5 Paul gave it a new depth of meaning. "Grace" represents God's special favor made available through Christ. For Paul, grace is almost synonymous with Jesus, for grace has become personalized in Christ. "Peace" clearly reflects the Hebrew idea communicated by the word *shalom*. It is the sense of spiritual well-being or wholeness that comes from a right relationship with God. For Paul, that relationship was procured for the believer by Christ's death on the cross.

Grace and peace come from "God our Father and the Lord Jesus Christ." It is important to note the clear association of Jesus Christ with God our Father. Further, notice the use of "Lord," which is the Greek form of the word used by translators of the Hebrew Bible to stand for the divine name (YHWH). When early Christians confessed at baptism "Jesus is Lord," they were affirming that Jesus was fully God. The linking of "grace" with *shalom* is important because the Galatians were in danger of choosing law over grace.

Paul then particularized Jesus as the one who gave Himself for our sins. Remember that in verse 1 Paul focused on the activity of the Father in raising Jesus from the dead. Notice in verse 4 that the Son gave Himself willingly as a sacrifice to remove our sins. Possibly Paul had in mind the sin offering of the Old Testament. It could also be that Paul had in mind the self-giving manner in which Jesus lived His entire life, and thus the reader would think of the Suffering Servant in Isaiah 53. In either case, Paul underlined the magnitude of Christ's sacrificial death for our redemption. While the Son's action was voluntary, it was one with the Father's desire. Thus, to belittle the work of the Son is to make light of the Father.

Our redemption is further described as a "rescue," which implies that people are in peril and cannot save themselves. In Christ we are rescued from this present evil age. The division between the present age and the age to come was familiar to every Jew. Throughout the New Testament the present age is depicted as being under the power of the evil one. The present age is hastening to a close and has nothing of eternal value. The rescue does not take us out of the world, but it places us in a new arena where Jesus is Lord. Practically it means that we can live in the present world with the perspective and power of God's kingdom.

For a Jew to follow any mention of the divine name and activity with a reverential blessing came naturally. The blessing "to whom be the glory forevermore" can be understood as a prayer or an affirmation. If taken as a prayer, Paul was exhorting God's people to ascribe to Him glory forever. If an affirmation, Paul was affirming that glory was a necessary trait of God. "Glory" describes the inexpressible and indescribable radiance or majesty of God. "Amen" signifies total agreement with the prayer. While Paul's opponents minimized Christ's redemptive work, Paul magnified it.

A Counterfeit Gospel Is No Gospel (vv. 6-9)

A counterfeit coin and a counterfeit gospel alike have no value; but in the case of the counterfeit gospel more is at risk—eternity itself lies in the balance. This deep concern prompted Paul to omit the traditional Eastern polite opening greetings and words of commendation. In verse 6 he expressed his shock with the strong word "amazed," which suggests that he was dumbfounded. It is not that the Galatians were in danger of swerving from a certain theological position; they were in danger of transferring their loyalty away from the one who gave Himself for their sins.

That this danger emerged "so quickly" implies that the Galatians' struggle had not been a long one where the false teachers had finally worn them down. The rapid turn could mean so quickly after their conversion or so quickly after the arrival of the false teachers. "Deserting" is in the present tense, indicating that the Galatians' possible desertion was an ongoing process and therefore it was not too late for them to return to the authentic gospel. The verb is also in the middle voice, indicating they are the ones responsible and therefore must return by an act of the will.

The issue at hand is not one of choosing against Paul in favor of the false teachers (1:10); the Galatian Christians were rebelling against the one who called them. They were not in danger of deserting a theological teaching but a personal loving God who called them by the grace of Christ. The call to salvation is the work of the Spirit who convicts us of sin and of the grace of Christ to forgive. "Called" is an aorist verb that indicates a decisive action requiring a total response. Divine sovereignty does not overrule human responsibility. Later in 5:10 Paul expresses his confidence that the Galatians would not be taken in by this counterfeit gospel.

Paul first calls it a "different gospel" (v. 6) and immediately affirms in verse 7 that it is "not another." He retracts the word "gospel" as a reference to that which is being taught by the Judaizers since there can be only one true gospel. The gospel leads to forgiveness and freedom; their bogus gospel would lead to bondage.

The source of the trouble was likely an extreme right-wing group of Jewish Christians who wanted Gentiles to submit to Mosaic law in addition to trusting Christ for salvation. They are often referred to as *Judaizers* by modern-day scholars. It is unlikely they would deny that salvation was through Christ; they would, however, indicate that faith in Christ was not enough. In addition, a person must obey the Mosaic law for salvation (see 3:1-3). Most heresy does not fully contradict the truth; it simply alters it.

Paul's response in verses 8 and 9 is direct and powerful, indicating the seriousness of the issue. No doubt some Galatian Christians had been awed by august figures from the mother church in Jerusalem who seemed to claim apostolic authority for their message. When this heresy was originally discussed at the Jerusalem Council (Acts 15:1-29), James disclaimed any official connection to the Judaizers. Paul thus includes himself and his companions, along with possible angelic messengers, to teach an important principle. The messenger's credentials (supposed or real) do not authenticate the message; the message validates the messenger. Many young people have been discouraged in their faith by college professors who sported their credentials as they distorted biblical teaching.

Paul pronounced that any messenger who distorts the gospel is under a curse. These strong words are not an angry outburst from Paul but a pronouncement of God's attitude toward any who would distort the gospel. Some commentators think that Paul may have been reminding the Galatians that Satan could appear as an angel of light. Others think Paul was speaking of a good angel. This seems more likely, since it is linked to Paul and his partners. The fact that Paul spoke of himself and a possible angelic messenger underlines the importance of accurate teaching when it comes to the gospel.

The repetition of the curse in verse 9 in an all-inclusive manner ("if *any* man," emphasis added) gives us a clear picture of the seriousness with which we must take doctrinal integrity. Paul repeated the warning because God's glory and the eternal welfare of souls were at stake. The singular "I" as opposed to the plural "we" in verse 8 may suggest that Paul was invoking his apostolic authority. In our day some might suggest that Paul was intolerant; but passages such as 1 Corinthians 9:19-23 indicate that Paul was very tolerant when it came to nonessential matters. The content of the gospel was not one of those.

Paul's Singular Desire (v. 10)

The Judaizers may have accused Paul of being a people pleaser, willing to modify his teaching to gain the favor of the crowd before him. They may have suggested that when he was speaking to Jews he preached the need for circumcision and law keeping to win their favor. Perhaps they accused him of doing so because he was insecure about his position as a "real" apostle. They may have said that when he preached to Gentiles, he would preach freedom from the law to win their favor. He was a sly politician rather than an authentic theologian, and thus he offered the gospel to the Gentiles at a discounted price.

Such untrue accusations would have troubled Paul greatly; however, the issue was not his own reputation but the truth of the gospel, which the Judaizers were distorting. Thus, Paul asked two rhetorical questions. The first asks whether Paul was trying to please man or God. The implied answer is God. The second question repeats in a slightly different manner the content of the first, and the answer is an unequivocal no. The very content of this letter to the Galatians, including the curses pronounced on the false teachers, shows Paul is no popularity seeker. In the coming section he will point to the opposition against him in Galatia as another clear indication that he did not compromise for the sake of popularity.

Paul's singular desire was to please Christ who saved him and called him, providing his apostolic authority. Here's the point: Paul said that because he was called by Christ and not by man (1:1), his original claim would be nullified if his goal was to curry the favor of humanity. This leads us to ask ourselves a few questions. As we encounter those who are without Christ, do we unapologetically declare the one true gospel? Does our desire to please others cause us to refrain from sharing the gospel?

For Memory and Meditation

"Grace to you and peace from God our Father and the Lord Jesus Christ, who gave Himself for our sins so that He might rescue us from this present evil age, according to the will of our God and Father." (Gal. 1:3-4)

The Freedom to Pray

"Jesus, I praise You for Your willingness to give Yourself to rescue me from sin and deliver me from the power of the pressures of this fallen world. In faith I accept Your promised freedom from the temptations that would enslave me."

Chapter 2

But God!

Galatians 1:11-24

Several years ago I wrote a series of devotional books on Kingdom promises. They all had two-word titles such as *He Is*, *We Can*, and *We Are*. The titles were chosen because a particular phrase was found in numerous Scripture passages. For example, every devotional in the *We Can* book was based on a verse that contained that phrase. The most well-known example is probably the one found in Philippians 4:13: "I can do all things through Him who strengthens me."

While I was working on the series, my wife and I were in the company of good friends of the family, Gary and Karolyn Chapman. Upon hearing of my new project, Karolyn encouraged me to add a book based on her favorite phrase in the Bible. When I inquired about the phrase, she responded with the two simple words—"but God!" She elaborated that throughout the Bible we find persons in difficult circumstances who are altered suddenly and dramatically by God's intervention. These are often preceded by the simple phrase—"but God!"

In writing to the Galatians, Paul had to explain his apostolic authority and calling in order to defend the essence of the authentic gospel. A group of false teachers, the Judaizers, wanted to add obedience to Mosaic law as a condition for salvation. They must have pointed out that Paul had not been with Jesus during His earthly ministry and had been a persecutor of the church. Paul didn't hide his past, nor did he glorify it. He stated, matter-of-factly, that he had been violent in his attempts to destroy the church and had been zealous for the ancestral traditions. His story was altered in a moment—"but when God" demonstrated His grace by revealing His Son—his worldview was altered completely.

A Revelation of Jesus Christ (vv. 11-12)

Paul was clear that his focus was not on himself but on the gospel that he had preached while in Galatia. The first issue he must clarify is that the gospel came directly from God through revelation. It was "not according to man. For I neither received it from man, nor was I taught it." The repetition in these first two verses indicates the seriousness with which Paul felt compelled to defend the gospel. The gospel was at stake, which had eternal consequences.

From Paul's defense we can surmise that some Judaizers had suggested that Paul was dependent on the apostles and elders in Jerusalem for approval and support. Paul thus provided corroborating evidence from his life and ministry. This brief account is not intended to be a complete autobiography; Paul selected the events that would support his main contention that his apostolic calling had come from the resurrected Lord. When he omitted an event mentioned elsewhere (i.e. Acts, or other Pauline letters), it was not an effort to deceive the Galatians. On the contrary, Paul ended the section with an oath confirming the truthfulness of his story (v. 20).

The "I" in verse 12 is emphatic, giving emphasis to the assertion that the gospel did not reach him through any human source. It was not transmitted from teacher to pupil. Its only source was "a revelation of Jesus Christ." This means it was identical in its source and content to that preached by any true apostle. Paul was called upon frequently to defend his apostolic credentials, since he had not traveled with Jesus as had the Twelve. In 1 Corinthians 15:8

Paul listed the Damascus road experience as one of the resurrection appearances. He considered himself as the last and least of the apostles because of his persecution of the church and his "untimely" birth. Nonetheless, he was an apostle by the grace of God.

As a student of Gamaliel (Acts 22:3) Paul would have been schooled in the Old Testament Scriptures that contained numerous messianic promises. As a persecutor of the church, Paul must have known many of the facts about Christ's life, teaching, and death. He was certainly aware of the claims that Jesus had been raised from the dead. After all, Paul had been an eyewitness to the stoning of Stephen and had heard Stephen pray to the Lord Jesus, requesting Him to receive his spirit (Acts 7:59-60). At the time, Paul considered such a statement to be blasphemous, and he became zealous to put an end to the followers of Christ.

No matter how detailed was Paul's knowledge of these events, they did not yet constitute the gospel. As a persecutor, he rejected the resurrection. He had failed to connect the many messianic promises with the life and teaching of Jesus of Nazareth. Only when light from heaven fell on Paul, and he heard the voice of the resurrected Lord, was everything altered. He then saw Jesus as the resurrected and exalted Lord. This personal encounter made all he had read in the Scriptures and all that he had heard and experienced come into clear focus.

Paul affirmed simply, "I received it through a revelation of Jesus Christ" (Gal. 1:12). Calling the gospel "a revelation of Jesus Christ" means that Christ was both the source and the content of the revelation. God is the source of all revelation, and its content is Christ. Paul knew many of the facts about the life and ministry of Jesus, but with the veil of unbelief removed from his eyes, Paul knew for certain that Jesus was the Christ and thus the only means of redemption. It is still true that no one can see the truth about Jesus without the illumination of the Holy Spirit.

But when God (vv. 13-16a)

Perhaps you have been asked to write your testimony based on three simple statements—life before Christ, receiving Christ, and life after Christ. You are in good company. That is precisely what Paul does in this section. The use of "former" in verse 13 tells us that in true conversion there is a former life that is now in the past.

No doubt the Galatians had heard about Paul's past by reputation and by his own testimony while in Galatia. It is also likely that the Judaizers had emphasized Paul's past in an effort to discredit him. It is instructive that Paul doesn't elaborate on the horrid details of his past as a persecutor. The word translated "persecute" indicates a practice extending over a period of time—a habitual practice. The same word is used in Acts 9:4 where Luke recorded Jesus's words to Paul on the Damascus road. The phrases "beyond measure" and "tried to destroy it" indicate excessive violence. When we give our testimony, there is no need to glorify our sinful past; we should mention it only as a backdrop to God's amazing grace.

Paul had attempted to destroy "the church of God." In this case "church" means the universal church made up of Jew and Gentile alike. The church is God's peculiar treasure. Further, an equivalent word is used in Old Testament days to speak of Israel as God's "peculiar treasure" (Ex. 19:5, KJV). As Paul learned on the Damascus road, opposition to the church was, in truth, opposition to Jesus Himself. For the Judaizers to stand against Paul and the revelation he received was to stand against God and His ongoing work of redemption through the church.

In Galatians 1:14 Paul also spoke of his zealous quest to excel in the "ancestral traditions." He had been a Pharisee, and his religious expression in the past had been based on works. Paul's use of the phrase "extremely zealous" indicates that he was never lukewarm. If a person compares religious commitment to a race, Paul was far ahead of all his competition. Such progress in a young rabbi would be demonstrated by increasing knowledge and practice of "ancestral traditions." By the time of the New Testament, the Law was being buried under the load of Jewish oral law that supplemented the written law. This was the law that marked the Pharisees, whom Jesus referred to as whitewashed tombstones (Matt. 23:27). An impossible works-based salvation had been created, and Paul was concerned for those who had fallen under the influence of the Judaizers.

Pay attention to the phrase "but when God" (Gal. 1:15). This is the moment everything changed for Paul. This is when the persecutor of the church became the preacher of the gospel. Paul was clearly speaking about his conversion experience on the Damascus road. Yet he began his story much earlier by indicating that God had set him apart from his mother's womb. Likely, this statement reflects the testimony of the great prophet Jeremiah (Jer. 1:5). From Paul's conception in the womb he was designed for his mission and ministry to the Gentiles. This verse speaks not only to the issue of the sanctity of human life; it speaks to the unique purpose and calling God has for everyone. You, like the great apostle, have been born with great potential for advancing God's kingdom.

The one, true God who created Paul in his mother's womb had called him through His grace. This emphasis on calling by grace has already been used in verse 6 to speak of the redemption experience of the Galatians under Paul's preaching. Paul narrated his conversion experience to show God's awesome power. He traced all the events of his physical and spiritual birth to God's sovereign activity. Nonetheless, Paul never denied the necessary response to divine activity. When he rehearsed this event before Herod Agrippa, he added, "I did not prove disobedient to the heavenly vision" (Acts 26:19). This balance of sovereign calling and obedient response motivated Paul to write this passionate letter to the Galatians, demanding a volitional response.

The immediate purpose of God's calling was "to reveal His Son" in Paul (Gal. 1:16). The use of "His Son" indicates that God was the source of revelation, and His Son was the content. God wanted Paul to know that Jesus, whom Paul was persecuting, was God's only Son, bearer of the very essence of God Himself. The event that occurred on the Damascus road was nothing less than a glorious manifestation of Jesus in a form that revealed Him as God's Son.

To reveal His Son "in me" is more than intellectual knowledge; it is heart knowledge that brings transformation (cf. 2 Cor. 3:18). Notice that Paul did not say "to me," but "in me," implying that when Christ is revealed to someone, the ultimate purpose is the revelation of God through that person. The revealing of God's Son to Paul found its ultimate purpose in Paul preaching the gospel to the Gentiles. "Among the Gentiles" could be translated as "among the nations," signifying all non-Jewish people. We should note that we can never separate calling unto salvation from calling to a task in God's kingdom.

The Persecutor Turned Preacher (vv. 16b-24)

The rather abrupt phrase "I did not immediately consult with flesh and blood" in verse 16 introduces Paul's discussion of his travel and ministry immediately following his conversion. The purpose of this section is to fortify his assertion that the gospel he preached was entrusted to him by Christ, as was the case with the Twelve. It is interesting that the phrase "flesh and blood" is the same phrase used in speaking of Peter's understanding of His messianic identity (Matt. 16:17).

Paul declared first that he did not go immediately to Jerusalem. Blinded by the heavenly light, he had been led by the hand to Damascus (Acts 9:8). There was no time for anyone to impose their subjective ideas on Paul. The rather emphatic "I did not... consult" indicates that his decision was based on his conviction that he was on equal terms with the apostles because he had seen the Lord and received the gospel directly from Him.

Paul went to Arabia first and then returned to Damascus. Acts doesn't mention this trip; but that is unimportant, since neither Luke nor Paul was writing a complete story of Paul's life. The Arabian visit was likely related to communion with God and future direction. Paul would have been fully aware of Old Testament Scriptures concerning the Messiah, and he knew that the early Christians had applied those Scriptures to Jesus. This was certainly a factor in his decision to attempt to destroy the church. Paul didn't need to go to Jerusalem; he needed to rethink his own position, and that required time alone with the Lord.

Three years passed before Paul went to Jerusalem. According to Acts 9:20-22 he had already been preaching effectively throughout Damascus, proving that Jesus is the Christ. His effective ministry had stirred up the Jews, and they bribed the ethnarch of Damascus into joining their plot to kill Paul. Paul escaped in a large basket and then headed to Jerusalem to become acquainted with Peter (vv. 23-26; Gal. 1:18). We would love to know the details of that meeting that lasted for slightly more than two weeks. We can imagine that Paul would have inquired about details of Jesus's life and ministry, the condition of the church in Jerusalem, and how he might work cooperatively with the other apostles. Whatever the case, they met as equals and co-laborers for the Kingdom.

Paul is quick to note that he did not meet with any of the other apostles during this time. We can only assume that the other apostles were not in Jerusalem. Possibly the growing hostility from Herod prompted some to leave (Acts 12:1-2). Likely many scattered Christian communities needed guidance to be supplied by the apostles. Paul mentions James, the Lord's brother, for the sake of total disclosure. James, like Paul, was not among the original apostles, and thus he would be an apostle in the more general sense of the term. Acts makes it clear that James quickly became prominent in the early church (12:17; 15:13).

The issue of apostolic authority, and thus the integrity of the gospel, is of such importance that Paul appealed to God as his witness. The phrase "before God" in Galatians 1:20 indicates that Paul was aware that every aspect of his life was lived in the very presence of God. Thus, God alone knew the events and motives behind the events.

Having recounted his brief visit to Jerusalem, Paul continued with the narration of his travels and ministry. He left Jerusalem and traveled to Syria and Cilicia. Damascus was the capital city of the province of Syria; Cilicia was the province of Paul's hometown, Tarsus. He must have served there until Barnabas brought him to Antioch (Acts 11:25-26). Galatians 1:21-24 covers a period of nearly fourteen years (cf. Gal. 2:1). The point of Paul's travel narrative is to show that his ministry was in remote areas where he had no contact with any of the original apostles.

Because of the area of his ministry, Paul was "still unknown by sight to the churches of Judea" (v. 22). The churches of Judea were composed of Christians scattered from Jerusalem as a result of persecution after Stephen's death (Acts 8:1). Some of them may have heard of Paul the persecutor, but Paul the missionary was personally unknown to them. Paul admitted that conversation about the persecutor turned preacher had spread widely (Gal. 1:23). The churches of Judea responded to this news by giving glory to God (v. 24).

Likely, Paul was contrasting the response of the churches in Judea with that of the Galatians. Those who "kept hearing" (v. 23) rejoiced about Paul's work, while the Galatians, who knew him personally, were being stirred to distrust by false teachers. In the phrase "preaching the faith," the word *faith* means the objective content of the gospel. If churches who were as Jewish as those in Judea could praise God for Paul, why were the Galatian Judaizers so critical of him?

The fact that Paul ended this brief defense with an emphasis on "glorifying God" is significant. Paul was not selfishly trying to defend himself. The very essence of the gospel was at stake, and for that reason Paul was willing to lay out the facts in order to defeat a falsehood. He was contending for "the faith" and for the faith of the Galatians.

For Memory and Meditation

"'He who once persecuted us is now preaching the faith which he once tried to destroy.' And they were glorifying God because of me." (Gal. 1:23-24)

The Freedom to Pray

"Father, thank You for changing me and giving me the freedom I once rejected. May others glorify You because of the change in me."

Chapter 3

Entrusted with the Gospel to the Gentiles

Galatians 2:1-10

Have you ever been entrusted with something precious? When I was a child, one of our neighbors sent word that he had purchased a Christmas gift for me. They lived just down the road from our house, but my dad determined that it was too dangerous for me to ride my bike on the busy rural road to obtain the package. My older brother was given the assignment of fetching the precious package for me. He returned a few moments later with the package, but the model truck inside was in pieces. He had accidentally dropped it on the ride home. As you might imagine, I broke into tears when I saw my precious gift in pieces. My brother, who at this stage did as much as possible to torment his younger brother, was clearly upset by his failure to deliver the package that had been entrusted to him. To my surprise, he spent the remainder of the evening attempting to reassemble the scattered pieces.

My brother was moved to action because he knew my dad had trusted him to deliver the package intact. The apostle Paul's actions throughout his ministry were based on his conviction that God had gifted and called him to share the gospel to the Gentiles. This sacred trust compelled him to endure countless challenges to his ministry.

CHAPTER 3

Paul's Return to Jerusalem (vv. 1-3)

No one wants to think his or her work might be in vain. The Great Apostle returned to Jerusalem after an interval of fourteen years to ensure the lasting value of his ministry to the Gentiles. But precisely what did Paul mean when he wrote "for fear that I might be running, or had run, in vain"? After all, he had just written of his firm conviction that God had set him apart and called him to minister to the Gentiles.

The fourteen-year period could start either with Paul's conversion or his first trip to Jerusalem. If we start with Paul's conversion, the total number of years would be seventeen, and the date would be approximately AD 50. If the first visit mentioned in 1:18 is indeed the one recorded in Acts 9:26, then this visit must be either the visit of Acts 11:30 (the famine relief visit) or the Council of Jerusalem (15:2). Bible scholars champion both views. If it is the Council of Jerusalem, then we must assume that Paul did not mention the famine-relief visit in this letter because it had nothing to do with theological matters. Note that neither Paul nor Luke, the author of Acts, was attempting to give a complete timeline of the movements of the apostle. Both men selected those events that were pertinent to the story the Holy Spirit inspired them to write.

Those who think Paul was referring to the famine visit (Acts 9:26) point out that it occurred before the first missionary journey. They argue that Paul would have wanted to have the issue of the conversion of the Gentiles settled before he began his work. Those who argue for the Council of Jerusalem believe it fits the timeline established by Acts and makes better sense of Paul's argument in the Galatian correspondence. The key issue, in either case, is that Paul makes a solid case that no man could have given him the gospel. His ministry had been well established before he "submitted to them the gospel which I preach among the Gentiles" (2:2). In either case, it seems likely that this letter was written soon after the Council of Jerusalem.

Paul's two companions on this visit were Barnabas and Titus. Barnabas, whose real name was Joseph, was a Levite from Cyprus. His generous act of selling land and giving the money to the apostles (Acts 4:36-37) earned him the nickname "Barnabas," meaning "son of encouragement." He soon came to have a leading role in the church of Jerusalem. When many persons were converted in Antioch, Barnabas was sent there as a representative of Jerusalem. Luke describes him as "a good man, and full of the Holy Spirit and of faith" (11:24). Barnabas had already risked his reputation by commending Paul (9:26-27), and he doubled down by calling him to be his associate in Antioch. They were partners on the first missionary journey (13:1-2).

Titus was a Gentile convert who may have been directly influenced to faith through Paul's ministry (Titus 1:4). He was a trusted servant and was especially involved in Paul's ministry to the churches in Corinth. Titus was a valued partner who assisted the Corinthians in completing (2 Cor. 8:6) and dispatching their contribution for the relief of the saints in Jerusalem. Paul spoke of Titus's earnest love for the Corinthians (vv. 16-17) and described him as Paul's "partner and fellow worker among you" (v. 23). Titus's presence is particularly important because he was a Gentile who was not required to be circumcised (Gal. 2:3).

The mention of the revelation that prompted Paul to make this return visit to Jerusalem indicates that God alone directed him. He was not responding to orders from "those who were of reputation" (v. 2), nor had he scheduled this visit on his own. On one occasion Paul received a direct revelation from God (Acts 16:9);

Chapter 3

in other cases God's directions were communicated through the gathered church (13:1-2) or another believer (11:27-30). Those who believe that this is the famine-relief visit identify this revelation with that of 11:28. The main point is that Paul was not reporting as a subordinate to his superiors. There is no indication that Paul had ceased, even for a moment, his preaching ministry until the Jerusalem leaders approved his message.

Why then did Paul submit to the Jerusalem leaders the gospel he preached among the Gentiles? At this point they could not alter the content of Paul's preaching. They could either accept it as genuine or reject it outright. Paul realized that the circumstances between his first visit and this later visit had been altered, and thus he had no qualms about going to Jerusalem and visiting with the leaders. At stake were the unity of the church and the full and unqualified acceptance of Gentiles as fellow believers. Paul knew that if the Jerusalem leaders undermined his work the effectiveness of his mission could be hindered greatly and the church could be divided. Such would mean that he had run in vain.

Titus is mentioned because the issue of the circumcision of Gentiles after conversion could cause division in the early church (Acts 15:1-29). Paul was aware his opponents might argue that he was inconsistent because he had Timothy circumcised (Acts 16:3). Timothy, however, had a Jewish mother; and circumcision would therefore enable him to have an effective ministry among Jews. Titus was a Gentile, and if the leaders had compelled him to be circumcised, they would fortify the idea that circumcision was necessary for salvation. If Titus was not compelled in a Jewish setting before those of reputation, then no Gentile male would be expected to be circumcised. Both Peter (Acts 15:10) and James (v. 19) would affirm this before the Council in Jerusalem.

The Truth of the Gospel (vv. 4-5)

Perhaps you think the whole matter of circumcision seems trivial as we read this text two thousand years later. Clearly, great damage has been done to local churches in our day over issues as trivial as carpet color or music style. But this was no trivial matter. At stake is "the truth of the gospel" (v. 5). Can a person be saved by grace alone through faith alone, or must some human achievement be added?

Paul believed the entire controversy was the result of "false brethren." The description in verse 4 implies that these persons had been sent by some outside party to sneak in and spy out the liberty being practiced by Gentile believers. The "false brethren" are sometimes referred to as legalists or Judaizers. Whatever the label, these persons believed a person could gain salvation by obeying Jewish laws and rituals.

Paul doesn't tell us who was responsible for planting these spies; but from the information gained from Acts 15, we can assert confidently that it was neither Peter nor James. We can surmise that it was a group of Jewish Christians who had once belonged to the Pharisaic party (Acts 15:5), or a large bloc of converted Jews who were still zealous for the law (cf. Acts 21:20). Paul used a strong word—"bondage"—in Galatians 2:4 to speak of their work and the grip of legalism. The Gentiles were slaves to the flesh and their own system of religion, but exchanging one form of slavery for another does not give a person liberty. The demands of the law were an unbearable yoke (Acts 15:10; cf. Gal. 5:1).

Paul's response was unyielding! Not for a moment did he consider compromise when the fate of Gentile converts and the truth of the gospel were at stake. Paul's steadfast stand convinced the Jerusalem leaders to support his viewpoint. Paul was ready to accommodate himself when the truth of the gospel was not at stake. For example, he was willing to enter the temple with those who had taken a Nazarite vow (Acts 21:17-26). The principle that we can learn is this: have flexibility in minor issues but do not compromise on the major issues.

Aware of the Grace Given to Me (vv. 6-10)

Paul concludes this section by pointing to the fruit of his life and ministry as the evidence of God's power and grace working through him. His conversation with the Jerusalem leaders did not result in any alteration in his gospel. On four different occasions in this section Paul describes the Jerusalem leaders as those of high reputation. Likely he is echoing the word of the Judaizers who have been "name-dropping" to make their case seem more credible. The Judaizers may have argued that Peter, James, and John were the pillars of the church, thus giving it stability (v. 9).

The phrase in verse 6 "what they were" may be a reference to the peculiar position of these three men during Jesus's earthly ministry. We can understand why early Christians gave deference to the early apostles and Jesus's earthly brothers. Paul's statement, "What they were makes no difference to me" should not be understood as disrespect for these men. He held them in high regard and met with them willingly. The strong emotion of the statement reflects Paul's disapproval of the comparison of his ministry and theirs. Since Paul had received his mission and commission from the exalted Christ, they were all fellow laborers. Paul added that God does not take human credentials into account. Aren't you glad He shows no partiality?

Not only did these men of reputation offer neither criticism nor correction, they recognized divine power at work in Paul's message and ministry. The phrase "on the contrary" in verse 7 marks a strong contrast. When these men heard the sound content of the gospel Paul preached, experienced his enthusiasm for his mission, and saw the results of his ministry, they recognized that his unique calling to the Gentiles was like that of Peter to the Jews. They knew that the two men may have used different methods, but they preached the same message in the same power (v. 8).

Peter and Paul had different mission fields, but that does not indicate their lack of concern for the Jews or Gentiles. Paul usually began his ministry by preaching in a local synagogue. Peter was the pioneer of ministry to the Gentiles, as God directed him to the home of Cornelius. For both men, the reaching of the lost meant more than a courteous agreement about fields of labor. The same should be true of us today.

I love the phrase "recognizing the grace that had been given to me" (v. 9). Paul frequently used the term "grace" (*charis*) to refer to his gifting and call to ministry. In Ephesians 3:8 he wrote: "To me, the very least of the saints, this grace was given, to preach to the Gentiles the unfathomable riches of Christ." The phrase "this grace" is explained earlier in verse 2: "If indeed you have heard of the stewardship of God's grace which was given to me for you." Luke tells us that when Barnabas arrived in Antioch, he witnessed the grace of God (Acts 11:23). No doubt Barnabas was referring not only to the influx of the Gentiles but also commenting on the fellowship exhibited in that community made up of Jew and Gentile.

The evidence of the powerful grace of God working through Paul prompted the "pillars" to give Paul and Barnabas "the right hand of fellowship." The right hand of fellowship was more than a friendly handshake; it was a sign of mutual agreement and acknowledgment. Paul's point is that these reputed pillars enthusiastically approved of him and his ministry. Only God could bestow and empower ministry, but their acceptance did give a "certain" accreditation to his work. It gave tangible evidence of unity, which prevented disruption in the early church.

The fact that Paul listed James first probably reflects James's important role in the Jerusalem church. The Lord's brother was not an apostle in the sense of the Twelve, but his position as the Lord's half brother and his wisdom gave him a unique platform. Paul was not reluctant to use the word "pillars" to refer to these three respected leaders. The ringing endorsement, signified by the right hand of fellowship, certifies these men were partners in ministry; they were not his superiors.

After accepting Paul and Barnabas in warm fellowship, the Jerusalem apostles urged them to continue remembering the poor (v. 10). The verb tense indicates Paul was already doing this. His early trip to Jerusalem described in Acts 11:27-30 was proof of his concern for the poor. "The poor" is not simply a reference to almsgiving; it was specifically related to the poor in Jerusalem. This one trip from Antioch was not the end of Paul's concern for the saints in Jerusalem. Paul discussed this collection in Romans and in 1 and 2 Corinthians. It was a major concern of Paul's throughout the decade of the fifties. It not only helped meet the needs of the saints, it legitimized the Gentile ministry and displayed God's grace.

This unique encounter of five men, who between them were responsible for twenty-one of the twenty-seven books in the New Testament, shows us that the New Testament is not a hodgepodge of conflicting theologies but a harmonious, beautifully variegated whole.[1]

For Memory and Meditation

But we did not yield in subjection to them for even an hour, so that the truth of the gospel would remain with you. (Gal. 2:5)

The Freedom to Pray

"Father, give me the courage not to yield to those who would cause me to compromise my freedom. May my witness make known the truth of the gospel."

---

[1] William Hendriksen, *New Testament Commentary: Exposition of Galatians* (Grand Rapids, MI: Baker Book House, 1968), 86.

Chapter 4

The Truth of the Gospel

Galatians 2:11-21

What issues do you consider to be nonnegotiable? Are there some things that you are simply unwilling to compromise, even if it could impact your job security and finances? I have talked to numerous persons in business who have had to make hard decisions they knew could affect their futures. For example, what if your boss told you it was necessary for you to deceive a client for the sake of a business deal? He or she made it clear that the deal was crucial for the future of the company, and the job security of several people lay in the balance. Would you rationalize that the ends justified the means? Or would you maintain your integrity?

Paul wasn't faced with a business decision, but he was faced with a dilemma that demanded he take a courageous stand. The church at Antioch is central to the entire Acts account as Luke recorded the work of the Spirit in advancing the Kingdom through the planting of churches. Antioch was the hub of the first-century church-planting movement.

While Paul was at Antioch, Cephas (Peter) came for a visit. In the beginning he welcomed the Gentiles who had responded to the gospel, and he demonstrated his welcome by joining in their fellowship meal. Such behavior was somewhat radical for a Jew who, at one time, had considered Gentiles to be unclean; but the Lord had given Cephas a vision that convinced him that God was not a respecter of persons (Acts 10:1-23). However, when certain men from Jerusalem came to Antioch, Cephas reversed course and held himself aloof (Gal. 2:11-12).

What was Paul to do? After all, he was an unknown quantity to many persons in the first-century church, and Cephas was one of the most respected leaders of the early Christian movement. Does he stand on conviction and confront Peter, or does he ignore the slight to the Gentiles? The decision was simple, because the truth of the gospel was at stake.

Sharing the Lord's Table (vv. 11-14)

I once wrote a small devotional book entitled *But God*. The adversative conjunction *but* introduces a change in events that transforms them from crises to opportunities to see God at work. The adversative verse 11 "but when" introduces an event that is contrasted with the positive response of the Jerusalem Council, which has just been recounted.

This event, while negative, demonstrates the essential independence of Paul's position and his gospel. This particular visit by Cephas (Peter) to Antioch is not chronicled in the Acts account, and therefore we can't be certain of the exact time of the visit. Whenever it occurred, it is clear that Peter stayed long enough for persons to observe his behavior.

When Peter arrived and witnessed the wonderful fellowship that Gentiles and Jews were enjoying as they ate together, he eagerly joined in the festivities. It is likely that the community meal (sometimes referred to as the love feast) concluded with the Lord's Supper. Since Peter ate the common meal with Gentiles, we can assume that he also partook of the Lord's Supper with these new brothers and sisters in Christ.

Peter altered his behavior radically when "certain men from James" arrived (v. 12). He withdrew and held himself aloof. He did not refuse to eat with Gentiles based on his own convictions but because he feared the party of the circumcision. Paul did not imply that James sent the men; indeed James denied having given any instructions to certain persons who were disturbing the Gentiles in Antioch. The name *James* is used to identify these persons with the church in Jerusalem where James was a noted leader.

Fellowship around the table both implies and requires a certain level of intimacy. In Corinth the issue that created a problem in the sharing of the table had to do with wealth (1 Cor. 11:17-22). In this instance the issue was racial and cultural as represented by the Jews and Gentiles. Jews were required to abstain from certain foods that were considered unclean (Lev. 11). Beyond that, for generations rabbis had expanded on the divine ordinances about food by adding laws regarding the washing of hands before eating, not based on hygienic reasons, but out of fear of being contaminated by contact with a Gentile. The "party of the circumcision" in Galatians 2:12—another way of referring to "certain men from James"—insisted that Gentiles must observe various Jewish regulations, which likely included rabbinic traditions related to clean and unclean.

Peter, like most modern-day believers, could be inconsistent in showing courage and standing on issues of conviction. We can point to his thrice-repeated denial of the Lord (Matt. 26:69-75; Mark 14:66-72; Luke 22:54-62; John 18:17-18, 25-27). Peter's cowardice impacted other Jewish Christians who followed his lead. Paul was clearly shocked and disappointed "that even Barnabas was carried away by their hypocrisy" (Gal. 2:13). Paul owed a great deal to Barnabas since he had risked his reputation by bringing Paul to Antioch (Acts 11:25-26). We might suggest that Barnabas did not want to offend the brethren from Jerusalem and thus decided that a brief abstention would not be a major issue.

Paul, however, saw it as a compromise that could split the early Christian community and create two Christian groups, existing side-by-side but unwilling to share the Lord's Table.

Paul saw this breach of fellowship as a denial of the truth of the gospel (Gal. 2:14). Everyone knew that Peter had received a special revelation on a housetop in Joppa that convinced him not to regard as "unclean" that which God had cleansed (Acts 10:9-16). He had acted boldly upon his vision and later gave a lengthy defense to the Jerusalem Council, which turned the tide concerning the legitimacy of the Gentile mission. Peter, by eating with the Gentiles, was living like them, and now his behavior was playing into the hands of the Judaizers who wanted the Gentiles to "live like Jews."

When we refuse to share the Lord's Table with another believer, our refusal suggests we consider ourselves to have something the other believer does not. Essentially we deny that person the full status of Christian, thus denying the very essence of the gospel.

Paul confronted Peter publicly because his behavior had caused others, including Barnabas, to join in gospel-denying behavior. The public refutation was thus appropriate and important. Paul addressed himself directly to the offender, which is always better than talking to others about him. Another point worthy of note is that Peter's acceptance of Paul's rebuke shows not only Peter's humility but indicates that the two men were on equal footing as apostolic leaders.

Justified by Faith (vv. 15-18)

In verse 15 Paul is referring to the common sentiment among Jews about their relative righteousness in comparison to Gentile sinners. Perhaps the Jews meant they were not guilty of the grosser vices directly prohibited by the law of Moses. It is noteworthy that Paul moves from "I" to "we," acknowledging his Jewish heritage. The clear sentiment is that highly privileged Jews were not like the coarse Gentiles. It is always easier to compare ourselves to someone we view to be less righteous than ourselves than it is to confront our own sin.

While this section may echo the essence of Paul's argument to Peter, the use of "we" throughout indicates that all "believing" Jews would of necessity concur with the logic of Paul's argument. By placing their faith in Jesus as the Messiah, Jewish believers had shown they understood that humans are not justified by the works of the Law. Christ, during His earthly ministry, made it clear that His message was not for the righteous but for those who were aware of their status as sinners (Matt. 9:13). In order to turn to Christ, the Jewish believers had first realized "that a man is not justified by the works of the Law."

The word *justified* occurs here for the first time in Paul's writings, and it appears four times in Galatians 2:16-17. The word is from the law courts and means "to declare righteous or innocent." Paul used it to speak of God's act of declaring righteous those who believe in Jesus Christ. "Faith in Christ Jesus" means a personal trust in Jesus for eternal life. Justification provides a right relationship with God that enables a believer to live righteously. The contrast presented by the phrase "works of the Law" (v. 16) indicates that it is impossible to win God's favor by keeping the commands of the Mosaic law, which would include all human works such as circumcision, dietary regulations, or Sabbath observances. Verse 16 ends with a loose paraphrase of Psalm 143:2, confirming that justification by faith was always God's plan.

In verse 17 Paul may be addressing the concern that the teaching of justification by faith might remove all incentive for moral behavior. If such were to occur, it would lead to a lower moral standard than living under the law of Moses. He concluded that if justification through faith in Christ leads to greater sin, it would be tantamount to saying that Christ is a minister of sin. Paul recoiled from such a blasphemous thought with utter horror—"May it never be!" That thought is utterly inconsistent with God's nature. Authentic faith in Christ involves a subsequent change in moral behavior that is produced by His Spirit indwelling us.

Paul concluded this section by using himself as an example. The very structure of human merit as a means of salvation was demolished by his encounter with the risen Christ on the Damascus road. Therefore, if Paul rebuilt a system of salvation by law-keeping, it would only serve to remind him again that he was a transgressor. The Law could only serve to demonstrate humanity's sin; it could not redeem us from our sin.

That I Might Live to God (vv. 19-21)

The final verses of chapter 2 are clearly Paul's testimony and must become that of every Christ-follower. If any person could have been saved by observance of the Law, it was Paul. Philippians 3 relates Paul's many accomplishments in Judaism, including his adherence to the Law. He was blameless based on human judgment, but never in the eyes of God. God's law demanded more than external righteousness; it required loving God with all a person's heart. No one, not even a rigorous Pharisee, could meet that requirement.

The Law can forbid, condemn, and judge. It can promote an awareness of sin and thus bring a sinner to the point of despair (cf. Rom. 7:12-13). For Paul, the Law demonstrated his abject sinfulness and rendered him a dead man, with the goal of leading him to life. The problem is not with the Law; it reflects God's perfect holiness. The problem lies with us. Paul died to the Law's requirement of perfect obedience in order that he might live to God.

Verse 20 describes Paul's conversion experience in graphic terms. He was crucified with Christ—as a dead man the Law no longer had any claim on Paul. This is the key section of Galatians; it declares the total sufficiency of the work of Christ for our salvation. The phrase "I have been crucified with Christ" uses a verb tense that indicates a definitive past action with continuing results. It speaks to a complete break with Paul's old life and his total way of thinking. He had labored throughout his life with the nagging fear that despite his religious zeal he might not be good enough, and a lifetime of accumulating merit would be wasted.

Christ fulfilled the Law perfectly; and yet, on the cross, He took upon Himself the consequences of humanity's sin. Encountering the risen Christ, Paul was forced to admit that he was a sinner just like the Gentiles. This was the final blow to his pride and self-esteem. Even though it was a death blow to his old way of thinking, it was his birth into a new life where Christ alone becomes the sole meaning of life.

Paul's life from that point was lived in total dependence upon the risen Christ. His relationship with Christ was so intimate and personal that he could speak of Christ living in him. Christ living in Paul gave him the motive and means of obedience. The righteousness he had attempted in vain to produce by human strength was now produced through him by Christ. Faith in God's Son, who loved Paul enough to give Himself up for him, gave purpose and power to Paul's life. The phrase "gave Himself up" points to the willing sacrifice of God's Son for all who will believe in Him.

After the passionate description of redemption in verse 20, verse 21 is a calm summary pointed at correcting the Judaizers.

Paul was saying to the Judaizers and those influenced by them that a definite choice must be made between salvation by grace, based on the death of Christ on the cross, and salvation by the law-works of humans. To follow the Judaizers was to declare this grace-act of God as invalid. By preaching the necessity of law-keeping, Judaizers were saying that what Christ did on the cross was not enough. If that were the case, "then Christ died needlessly."

It would be inappropriate to conclude this text without asking each reader to consider whether you are depending on your own merit to make you right with God. If so, why not pause and acknowledge your sin and appropriate the forgiveness that was purchased for you on the cross. Salvation is by Christ alone, by faith alone.

For Memory and Meditation

"I have been crucified with Christ; and it is no longer I who live, but Christ lives in me; and the life which I now live in the flesh I live by faith in the Son of God, who loved me and gave Himself up for me." (Gal. 2:20)

The Freedom to Pray

"Jesus, I believe that You now live in me, and You provide the strength that enables me to live in true freedom. I live as a free person by faith in the Son of God."

Chapter 5

The Gospel Is Not a Scam

Galatians 3:1-14

I am writing this while on quarantine during the rapid spread of COVID-19. The threat to our nation and communities has created an atmosphere where most people are working together for the good of the country and the health and safety of others. However, there are some persons who have seized upon this moment to make money, no matter the consequences to those in need. They are the scam artists who are making outlandish offers by e-mail or phone to unsuspecting and naïve persons. They make promises that seem too good to be true. And like our parents said, "If it sounds too good to be true, it probably is."

In the case of the Galatians, the reverse is true. The Galatian believers had become followers of Christ and thus had received the Spirit through the gospel of grace that declared that Christ had died in their place to pay the penalty of their sin. The Judaizers, first-century scam artists, were insisting that the simple gospel wasn't enough and that the Galatian believers needed to add works of the Law to their résumé in order to be truly saved.

This dangerous heresy prompted Paul to write with passion. If his concern was simply to defend his apostolic authority, he could have closed the epistle at the end of chapter 2. But Paul knew that more was at stake than his personal reputation; the issue at hand had eternal consequences. How can sinful man have a personal relationship with a holy God? In other words, how can humans be saved from the consequences of their own willful rebellion?

Chapter 5

Knowing that his opponents were likely to attempt to prove their case by appealing to the Old Testament scriptures, Paul turned his attention to the same body of Scripture. They were pointing to centuries of history and the proud law of Moses for their authority. Paul went further back in the story of redemption history to God's covenant with Abraham to prove his case that relationship with God was and is established by faith. Abraham, prior to the giving of the Law, "believed God, and it was reckoned to him as righteousness" (3:6).

Hearing with Faith (vv. 1-5)

Notice that Paul did not accuse the Galatians of gross sin; he accused them of being foolish. The word translated "bewitched" in the New American Standard Bible has the same root as the English word *fascinated*. Likely these young Gentile believers had been overwhelmed by the status and seemingly well-reasoned arguments by these men who claimed the authority of the mother church in Jerusalem. At some point you may have been approached by someone from a false religion who attempted to overwhelm you with his or her crafty use of Scripture taken out of context. If so, you can identify with the Galatian believers.

Paul was horrified that the Galatians were tempted to exchange his clear presentation of the gospel for an impossible works-based salvation. The phrase "publicly portrayed" alludes to Paul's clear presentation of the gospel, which led to their conversion. It was like a modern-day billboard so large and visible that no one can miss the message. As we study the text, you will notice that Paul asked questions in five consecutive verses. The answer to these questions should have enabled the Galatians to stand firm for the gospel. The first question is "who has bewitched you?" Not Paul—his message was clear and unmistakable—Christ crucified.

The second question (v. 2) asks about how the Galatians began their Christian pilgrimage—"Did you receive the Spirit by the works of the Law, or by hearing with faith?" Notice that the reception of the Spirit is associated directly with hearing the gospel and the corresponding response of faith. There is no suggestion that the reception of the Spirit is associated with the laying-on of hands or the act of water baptism, or that it occurs at some time after conversion. The convicting work of the Spirit enables us to respond in faith to the message of the gospel.

You may recall that the reception of the Spirit convinced Peter and the circumcised believers who were with him in Caesarea that Cornelius and other Gentiles had been saved by God's grace. Peter's message there was one of unlimited atonement: "Everyone who believes in Him receives forgiveness of sins" (Acts 10:43). While Peter was still speaking, the Holy Spirit fell upon those who were listening (v. 44). The believers were subsequently baptized as outward evidence of their response to the gospel (v. 48).

Peter later testified to the church at Jerusalem that the Spirit fell upon the Gentiles the way it did upon the Jewish believers in the beginning (Acts 11:15). He recalled in verse 16 that Jesus had promised that He would baptize people with the Holy Spirit and concludes: "Therefore if God gave to them the same gift as He gave to us also after believing in the Lord Jesus Christ, who was I that I could stand in God's way?" (v. 17). Paul consistently taught that all believers receive the Holy Spirit at conversion (cf. Rom. 8:9).

The simple answer to a simple question is that the Galatians had received the Spirit by hearing with faith. In fact, until the Judaizers came to Galatia, the Galatians had no knowledge of the necessity of following the ritual law as advocated by these false teachers. How were they saved? Through the simple act of hearing and believing (cf. Rom. 10:14-17). Galatians 3:2 contains a great lesson for us. One antidote to present spiritual wandering is to remember God's past actions in our lives.

Paul then posed a follow-up question in verse 3: "Having begun by the Spirit, are you now being perfected by the flesh?" Since the spiritual journey began by faith, does it seem logical that the ongoing process would occur through the flesh? The word *flesh* is used to provide a strong contrast with *Spirit*. "Flesh" means the works of humans rather than the supernatural work of the Spirit. "Being perfected" is a reference to the ongoing work of the Spirit as He conforms us to Christ. This work is often referred to as *sanctification* and will continue until we are present with the Lord.

The question in verse 4 may be interpreted two different ways. The word translated "suffer" can refer to physical sufferings or simply to experiences of life, whether good or bad. If physical sufferings, it means that the Galatians had been persecuted by their own countrymen because of their simple act of faith in believing in Jesus for salvation. If they turned from that simple gospel to a works salvation, it would mean that their suffering had been in vain.

Likely the Galatians had suffered; but that doesn't seem to be the point here, and it breaks the obvious flow of the passage. Verses 3 and 5 both speak of the blessings received as a result of their belief. The verb translated "suffer" (v. 4) in the New American Standard Bible is neutral and means "to experience." The New International Version translates, "Have you experienced so much in vain—if it really was in vain?" If the Galatians turned from grace to works, it would negate the blessings of the Spirit they had received through faith. The parenthetical phrase—"if indeed it was in vain" (NASB)—indicates Paul's confidence that the Galatians were wavering but had not abandoned their original position.

The final question in verse 5 relates to the Galatian believers' basis for having received the Spirit. Did they receive the Spirit at conversion by doing what the law required, or by believing the gospel? "Miracles" likely refers to the spiritual gifts that God gives to enable us to serve effectively and the fruit that enables us to live in community productively. In verses 1-5, Paul makes two things abundantly clear. Salvation comes by grace alone by faith alone, and all believers receive the Spirit at conversion.

Abraham, the Believer (vv. 6-9)

The Judaizers appealed to the law of Moses and may have been bragging about their descent from Abraham, as if this biological connection gave them higher rank and greater authority. This section begins with Abraham, and the next section will conclude with him (v. 14). Paul makes his case by quoting Genesis, Leviticus, Deuteronomy, and Habakkuk. Two things will be made abundantly clear: (1) God chose the Jewish nation to receive a blessing and, in turn, become a blessing to the nations; (2) the means of receiving and sharing that blessing was faith and not works.

Jews were interested in knowing how Abraham found favor with God. Paul referred to an incident in Genesis 15:6 to prove that it was because of Abram's faith that God counted him as righteous. That same chapter recounts a moment when Abram realized that God's promise of a son and multitudes of people was clearly impossible in the flesh. Abram, in absolute surrender, declared that God is Lord (v. 2). When Abram indicated that his only heir was his servant Eliezer, God showed him the heavens and told Abram that his descendants would be as numberless as the stars. Abram had no recourse but to believe God. Paul used this same verse in Romans 4:3 and 10 to make a similar argument about faith alone. Jesus also was clear that He was present in Abraham's faith (John 8:56).

Abraham, like the Galatians, had experienced God's blessing by realizing he could do nothing in his own fleshly strength to merit God's favor. He threw himself unreservedly on God, counting on Him to do that which he could not do for himself. The word translated "reckoned" is from the commercial world of accounting. God, in His grace, credited righteousness to Abraham's account without any merit on his part.

The Judaizers may have taught that God owed righteousness to Abraham because of his works. If they were arguing that circumcision was one of the works of the law necessary for salvation, then this passage is particularly pertinent to Paul's argument. Abraham was counted as righteous before his own circumcision, which is recounted in Genesis 17:23-27.

Paul then affirmed that only those who practice Abraham's response of faith are true sons of Abraham. Paul lifted the idea of sonship with Abraham to a new level. It is not mere biological or physical descent that matters, but spiritual likeness in terms of faith. Even Paul could be a Hebrew of the Hebrews and still not be a son of Abraham in the spiritual sense (cf. Phil. 3:5). This idea should not be a new one to the Judaizers. Jesus taught the same thing (Luke 19:9; John 8:39-40). Ironically the Judaizers, by relying on works, would disqualify themselves from being sons of Abraham.

Paul then went back even further in the story of Abram, recounting the very moment the original covenant was instituted by God. The phrase "the Scripture, foreseeing" in verse 8 is a normal Jewish form of speech. It means the same as "the Lord, foreseeing." What Scripture foresees, the Lord foresees; what Scripture says, the Lord says. Since the Holy Spirit inspired the writing of Scripture, God and His Word cannot be separated. While the inspiration and inerrancy of Scripture was not Paul's emphasis at that moment, this verse certainly affirms this great doctrine.

What was "foreseen," and thus determined before creation, was the means of redemption for all—Jew and Gentile alike—through faith and not works (cf. Eph. 1:4, 11). What did Paul mean when he said "preached the gospel beforehand?" In one sense, no Christian would speak of the gospel being complete before Jesus's death on the cross. In another sense, Abraham's response was an anticipation of the gospel. We might compare this phrasing to John 8:56, where Jesus spoke of Abraham having seen His day and responded with gladness.

Thus, in verse 9, Paul refers to Abraham as "the believer." Those persons whose faith is ongoing are blessed with Abraham. Paul made this very same argument in Romans 4. True descendants of Abraham are not those trying to earn God's favor but those who believe in God's promises, as did their father Abraham.

Christ Redeemed Us from the Curse (vv. 10-14)

Paul may have anticipated the unvoiced objection, "Why talk about Abraham, when the issue is the law of Moses." Paul again appealed to Scripture, this time beginning with Deuteronomy 27:26, a book penned by Moses. In verses 10-11 Paul shows the impossibility of fully carrying out God's demands in the law. If a person desired to be justified by the law, he or she would have to give full and complete obedience to all of God's demands. If we obey all the laws but one, we are still guilty of breaking them (James 2:10). Humanity's inability to obey the entire law brings everyone under a curse.

Some Rabbis employed great ingenuity trying to prove that the patriarchs had kept the law, even though it had not yet been given. They also taught that common folk who had neither knowledge of nor interest in the law were under God's curse. When a dispute arose regarding Jesus's identity, the officers inquired of the chief priests and Pharisees regarding their opinion. They affirmed: "No one of the rulers or Pharisees has believed in Him, has he? But this crowd which does not know the Law is accursed" (John 7:48-49). Paul turned the tables on those who would argue that Gentile sinners were under God's curse, demonstrating that all humanity, even Jewish scholars, were under the curse of the law.

Deuteronomy 27:26 is found at the very end of the curses spoken from Mount Ebal and prior to the blessings given from Mount Gerizim. The curse falls upon all who do not confirm the law to "perform them." The law was given to show humans the impossibility of living according to the entire law. Later, in Galatians 3:24, Paul will make a positive affirmation, arguing that the law serves as a custodian to lead us to Christ so that we may be justified by faith. The Judaizers were perverting the true purpose of the law by teaching that humans must obey it in order to be saved.

Paul's opponents were diverting the law from its true purpose. Their attempt was bound to result in tragic failure, because the law does not have the power to subdue a human's sinful desires. Verse 11 quotes Habakkuk 2:4 to confirm that no one is justified by the law. In its original context, the prophet wondered aloud why the unrighteous Chaldeans were swallowing up a people more righteous than themselves (Hab. 1:13). God answered:

> "Behold, as for the proud one,
> His soul is not right within him;
> But the righteous will live by his faith." (Hab. 2:4)

Habakkuk tells us what a righteous person is not— "the proud one"—before he declares what he or she is. Rather than relying on personal resources to achieve a certain style of life, he or she trusts solely on God. The wicked Chaldeans would not live; only the righteous live. The righteous are those who are justified by their faith in God. Paul also used the Habakkuk reference in Romans 1:17 to illustrate his doctrine of justification by faith. The truth that the righteous live by faith applies equally to persons in the Old and New Testaments and to Jews and Gentiles alike.

Verse 12 contains a quotation from Leviticus 18:5 to show that obeying the law as a means of earning God's favor is not an act of faith. The law required *doing* and not *believing*. The gospel demands faith in Christ; the law demands deeds. Leaning on the law means leaning on self, whereas exercising faith means leaning on God. By connecting these verses Paul indicated that complete obedience, even if it were possible, could not earn salvation.

Christ's obedience unto death brought hope and life where none existed. He redeemed us from the curse of the law. To explain how Christ became a curse for us, Paul quoted Deuteronomy 21:23. In its original context it refers to the practice of hanging the body of a condemned criminal on a tree of shame. Hanging the corpse of the guilty person on a tree added a measure of public disgrace.

The word "redeemed" introduces the ransom metaphor, which Paul used in Acts 20:28 in his message to the Ephesian elders (cf. 1 Pet. 1:18-19). Our failure to keep the law brought us under the curse of the law. Christ "redeemed us from the curse" we rightly deserved by "having become a curse for us" (Gal. 3:13). Christ paid the ransom price for our sin by His death on the cross. Jesus, who was without sin, paid the debt that we owed. He willingly bore the curse for us.

Then Paul stated the purpose for which Christ willingly bore our curse. Through His death, the blessing of declared righteousness promised to Abraham was made available to the Gentiles.

The promise to Abraham finds its ultimate fulfillment only in terms of Jesus Christ and His redemptive work on the cross. Notice the use of "we" in the last half of verse 14, which means that Paul, a Jew, was redeemed in the same manner as Gentiles. The death of Christ enabled *everyone* to receive "the promise of the Spirit through faith." This is the third time in this chapter (vv. 2, 5) that Paul referred to the gift of the Spirit as evidence of salvation.

Tina Boesch, in *Given: The Forgotten Meaning and Practice of Blessing*, says: "Jesus, the source of blessing and the author of life, became the curse—the representative of Israel's exile and our alienation from God. Christ didn't just die on the cross; he took the whole weight of the curse of sin and death into his own body."[1]

For Memory and Meditation

"Christ redeemed us from the curse of the Law, having become a curse for us." (Gal. 3:13a)

The Freedom to Pray

"Thank You, Lord, for redeeming me from the curse caused by my sinful inability to obey Your law. Teach me that I can now obey freely by the power of Your Spirit living in me."

---

[1] Tina Boesch, *Given: The Forgotten Meaning and Practice of Blessing* (Colorado Springs: NavPress, 2019), 184.

Chapter 6

An Irrevocable Covenant

Galatians 3:15-29

My wife's mom recently graduated to heaven at the age of ninety-six. She was prepared in more ways than one. Her personal relationship with the Lord was solid. She frequently told friends and family members that she was ready for the Lord to take her home. She had given certain special items to her children, grandchildren, and great-grandchildren. She had written out notes of her wishes for her own funeral service. She had secured an up-to-date will that provided specific and unalterable directions for the distribution of all her property. Her will had been properly executed and thus served as an irrevocable agreement that could not be set aside or amended by any of her heirs.

In this chapter's focal passage Paul continues his argument about the priority of salvation by grace through faith over obedience to the law by showing that God's promises preceded the giving of the law and thus had precedence as an irrevocable agreement.

The Promise to Abraham and His Seed (vv. 15-18)

Paul addressed the Galatians in verse 15 as "brethren," which is both courteous and intimate. He utilized a human analogy based on a custom with which they would have been familiar.

When a person establishes a legal contract, such as a last will and testament, it can neither be ignored nor altered by a third party. However, it seems likely that the Judaizers were arguing that the law annulled the earlier arrangement made with Abraham. Paul's point is that God promises righteousness by faith (Gen. 15:6), and He would not alter the terms of that agreement nor could any other party. Being in the form of a covenant, which was ratified by God and in force, it was not set aside by the law, which came later.

Paul's thesis about the earlier covenant still having precedence continues in verse 17, but first he paused to explain that the promise was not simply given to Abraham but to "Abraham and to his seed" (v. 16). The first point to note is that Abraham is not the only beneficiary of the covenant; his "seed" is also named as future beneficiary. You probably noticed Paul's emphasis on the singular nature of the word *seed*.

In the original account in Genesis, the singular seed was Isaac, the son of promise. If you read the original narrative of Abraham's faith journey, you will find that he offered first to adopt Eliezer, his servant (Gen. 15:1-6). God affirmed that the child of promise would come forth from Abram's own body. Later, Sarai suggested that Abram have a child through her handmaiden. Ishmael, the child born through this fleshly arrangement, was not to be the child of promise (ch. 16). Then in Genesis 17:19 God reaffirmed the promise of a son and an "everlasting covenant for his descendants after him."

Paul, however, interpreted the singular "seed" as having its ultimate fulfillment in Christ. His point was to affirm that Abraham and his descendants ultimately inherited the blessings of this irrevocable promise through the Messiah. When the Jews claimed special authority because of their Abrahamic lineage, Jesus responded, "Your father Abraham rejoiced to see My day, and he saw it and was glad" (John 8:56). The writer of Hebrews similarly affirmed that Abraham died in faith without receiving the promises, "but having seen them and having welcomed them from a distance" (Heb. 11:13b). We can rightly ask if the prophecy of Genesis 3:15, where God promised that the "seed" of the woman would bruise the head of the serpent, was not also in mind.

In verse 17 Paul returns to his former argument about the priority of the Abrahamic covenant. It is possible that the Judaizers were arguing that the law replaced the earlier promise because it was for Abraham alone. Paul insisted that the regulations the Judaizers were trying to force on Gentile believers came 430 years later than the covenant previously ratified by God. The point is clear: if a covenant ratified by humans could not be altered, how much less one ratified by God!

The 430-year time period is taken from Exodus 12:40. Some liberal scholars, predictably, see a possible conflict in the reference to 400 years in Genesis 15:13 and the 430 years mentioned in Exodus. Jewish rabbis also noticed the difference and solved the problem by suggesting the Israelites spent 400 years in Egypt, and 430 years was the time between God's covenant with Abraham and Moses' reception of the law. Note that the covenant is repeated and confirmed in identical language in God's promises to Abraham (Gen. 22:18), to Isaac (26:4), and to Jacob (28:14). If Paul was measuring the time from Jacob, that would also account for the 430 years.

The logical conclusion of the argument is critical to the issue facing the Galatian believers. If the inheritance is contingent on obedience to the law, then it is not based on the promise given to Abraham (Gal. 3:18). Such a conclusion would go against the very purpose of God in giving the promise, since *law* and *promise* are opposites and thus cannot be combined. It would suggest that works and grace were equal sources of eternal promises for God's people. If the promise was based on law, then only the people of the law could receive it, thus shutting out the Gentiles.

God's promise is an "inheritance," which means the enjoyment of the benefits already promised under the will. The word translated "granted" is from the same family from which the Greek word *grace* comes. It is also in the perfect tense, suggesting that the gift of salvation to Abraham was permanent. If the promise was received as a gift of grace, then it can never be achieved by meritorious work on our part. Salvation is God's gift and not man's achievement.

The Law Added because of Sin (vv. 19-22)

Paul's emphasis on the priority of the promise raises a critical question—why then was the law given? Paul's answer is both simple and straightforward: "It was added because of transgressions" (v. 19). No Jew in Paul's day would have thought of the law as being "added," but God's activity in saving Paul by grace had revolutionized Paul's thinking about how a person obtains righteousness. In his testimony as recorded in Philippians 3:9, Paul speaks of gladly exchanging his attempt to achieve righteousness by obedience to the law for one that comes from God based on faith.

The word *transgression* provides a word picture of people knowingly and intentionally stepping away from God's will. For that reason, the law was given to bring about in the hearts and minds of humankind the awareness of their sinfulness and guilt. The law could reveal God's righteousness, but it could not provide the power for humans to achieve it. It could reveal the problem of sin but not provide the power for humans to overcome it. The law is like light flooding in the window; it doesn't increase the amount of dirt in the room, but it makes it more visible.

God Himself gave the promise to Abraham, while the law was given to Moses by angelic messengers and then, in turn, mediated to the people by Moses. John's Gospel makes a similar contrast:

"For the Law was given through Moses; grace and truth were realized through Jesus Christ" (1:17). The Jewish belief in angelic communication of the law is shown in Stephen's speech (Acts 7:53) and may be the point of Hebrews 2:2. The law was not only inferior to the promise, having been given through mediation; it was also temporary as contrasted with the promise. The law had a period of duration and served "until the seed would come." Until Christ came and gave new life and the indwelling Spirit, humans had neither the moral pattern nor power to avoid sin.

Verse 20 continues to contrast the direct nature of the promise with that of the mediatorial nature of the law. Even though a mediator is important, he is only a third party acting between two other parties. Moses, the mediator, served as a link between God and people, lacking independent authority. The affirmation "God is only one" not only reflects the historic conviction of Jews (the Shema, Deut. 6:4), it affirms that God gave the promise to Abraham and his seed directly and personally based on His own sovereign design.

Paul then addressed another anticipated objection in verse 21: "Is the Law then contrary to the promises of God?" Paul's strong response, "May it never be!" indicates that such a suggestion was blasphemous. The law itself was not at fault; it reflects God's holiness and therefore would never contradict His promises. The law revealed God's righteousness and man's sin, but it could not impart life. If the law could have given life, then there would have been no reason for the death of Christ.

The word "Scripture" in verse 22 is a reference to the Old Testament, especially the sections of the law. Throughout Scripture humans are presented as sinners by nature and by practice. Paul used the imagery of a prison to picture the law. We are imprisoned by our own sin, and the law is our jailor. We are hemmed in on every side without any possibility of escape.

The Law, Our Tutor (vv. 23-24)

Paul may have anticipated another question: what purpose does the law serve? In verse 23 the phrase "before faith came" means the possibility of salvation by faith in Christ. Rather than the image of a jailor, Paul spoke of the law in terms of a custodian. In a sense Israel was under the the law's protective custody. The law taught Israel to worship the one, true God. In so doing, it shielded Israel from the idolatry of surrounding nations.

The law served the valuable purpose of preparing both Jew and Gentile for the wonderful gospel of justification by faith alone. Old Testament saints looked forward to the coming Redeemer who would save them by grace through faith alone, while Paul and his hearers could look back to the Redeemer who came in the flesh. The word "revealed" points to God's prior act of revelation that enables humans to believe in Him. For that reason, even our belief in Him is not a meritorious work on our part (Eph. 2:8). Thus, the law had a positive purpose, but it was temporary and inferior to faith in Christ.

Paul then took the analogy a step further, speaking of the law as "our tutor to lead us to Christ" (v. 24). Today, tutor refers to someone who teaches, but in Paul's day a tutor had a supervisory work, which often including disciplining. Wealthy Greek and Roman families often had tutors who would supervise their children from ages six through sixteen. The tutor would escort the children to and from school and watch over their conduct throughout the day. The law as tutor was intended "to lead us to Christ." Now that Christ has come, we have come of age and are no longer under a tutor.

One in Christ (3:25-29)

The implication of the preceding argument is now made clear. What a glorious thought: "For you are all sons of God through faith in Christ Jesus" (v. 26). We are no longer immature children under a tutor, but we are mature children with all the rights and privileges pertaining thereto. Tragically, the Judaizers were clinging to their tutor and were attempting to influence Gentiles who had never been under a tutor to join them in this bondage.

The reference to baptism in verse 27 is likely intended to remind the Galatian believers of their physical baptism when they demonstrated their death to self and new life in Christ. Paul's use of "all" shows that Jews and Gentiles are on equal standing. Baptism is the means by which believers confess their new relationship to Christ. The physical act of baptism does not create the union with Christ, but it does express it. Those who attempt to argue that baptism is necessary for salvation will find no help from this passage. If that were the case, baptism would fall into the same category as the circumcision and law-keeping the Judaizers promoted.

The phrase "clothed yourselves with Christ" graphically and intimately describes the union believers have with Christ. It may have derived in early Christian circles from undressing before baptism and then donning clean white clothing afterward.

The image is a very appropriate one to describe the total transformation of life where one lays aside the old self with its behavior patterns and puts on the new self "which in the likeness of God has been created in righteousness and holiness of the truth" (Eph. 4:24).

Since all were baptized into Christ, all share equally in His body. The first half of verse 28 shows the categories that have been removed, and the second half explains the basis for this new reality. The radical nature of this verse cannot be overstated. Jews drew a sharp line of separation between themselves and outsiders of heathen nations, often referring to them simply as dogs. Even proselytes were not given full status, since they were not children of Abraham.

But dividing walls were not found simply between Jews and Gentiles. Daily a pious Jewish male thanked God he was not a Gentile, a slave, or a woman. "In Christ," distinctions of race, social standing, and gender lose their significance. No one has greater or lesser blessings regarding salvation than anyone else who belongs to Christ. Everyone who is in Christ finds a new oneness that destroys all former divisions and injustices. They are all equal inheritors of His salvation. In Paul's day women and slaves had almost no rights. Paul's words struck a blow for spiritual freedom that had and continues to have far-reaching repercussions.

Verse 28 does not suggest that in Christian fellowship there are no racial, social, or sexual differences. Nor does it mean that Paul saw no distinctions between the functions of the different sexes in the roles in family and church. We are different because we are all uniquely created by God. However, these differences no longer hinder fellowship with God or others in His family.

The grand conclusion shatters all the arguments of the Judaizers who insisted that Gentile believers adopt a lifestyle of obedience to ceremonial law so they could claim a relationship to Abraham. Paul affirmed that all persons who belong to Christ are Abraham's descendants. It is not a matter of physical birth as a Jew but spiritual birth in Christ that matters. We are all "heirs according to the promise" (v. 29). Abraham was saved based on God's promise fulfilled in Christ, and all who will join him as heirs will be saved based on that same promise.

For Memory and Mediation

"But the Scripture has shut up everyone under sin, so that the promise by faith in Jesus Christ might be given to those who believe." (Gal. 3:22)

The Freedom to Pray

"Father, thank You that I have believed by faith in Your only Son. Give me the courage to live out my freedom in community as I relate to others who are different from me."

Chapter 7

Crying "Abba! Father!"

Galatians 4:1-20

When I was in junior high, a teenager in our school inherited a large sum of money. The news spread quickly in our small town and her popularity soared. While we were a little young for dating and pairing up, many of the guys were making plans to help her spend her money for a lifetime. Over time, interest among the guys began to decline because it became clear she didn't have access to the money. Her vast estate was controlled by a guardian until she reached a set age of maturity.

In this section Paul uses the imagery of a guardian to explain the value of the law, which served as guardian and manager until the date set by the father. During the time of guardianship, the child has no more rights than a slave. Yet the good news is that the time established by the heavenly Father has come to fulfillment, and God sent His own Son so that we might become full heirs and children.

Sons and Heirs (vv. 1-7)

In the last section Paul introduced the idea of the law being a tutor to lead persons to Christ. The phrase "now I say" in verse 1 indicates that he is continuing the idea of guardianship but now explaining what happens when the guardianship period comes to an end. In this first section Paul outlines two privileges that emerge from the new relationship to Christ that is now enjoyed by his readers. First, Christ gives the release from spiritual bondage (vv. 1-3); and, second, He provides the spiritual freedom implicit in sonship (vv. 4-7).

The word "heirs" (v. 1) is repeated from 3:29 and explains what is meant by the phrase "heirs according to promise." The comparison of an underage child with a slave may sound odd to our ears, but it is used to indicate the lack of rights the young child had in Paul's day. The father could determine the age at which a child would receive his or her inheritance.

The word "child" is used to identify anyone who has not reached the age of adulthood. This is essentially a contrast of Judaism and the fulfillment of its promise in the coming of Christ. Believers who desired to follow Jewish laws were returning to a status like children under guardians and stewards, not sons and heirs.

The reason the child is no better off than a slave in terms of "ownership" is that he or she "is under guardians and managers until the date set by the father" (v. 2). "Guardian" refers to the official who cared for the minor child's personal affairs. "Manager" was someone who handled the child's property. Thus Paul was no longer using the image of a tutor (cf. 3:25). Under Roman law a child came of age when he reached fourteen, but the law gave some discretion to the father's wishes.

The use of "we" in verse 3 allowed Paul to identify with believers in Galatia. "Children" refers to one's pre-Christian experience. In this case the children were not viewed as being under managers and guardians but "held in bondage under the elemental things of the world." "Elemental things" may mean elementary religious teachings or possibly evil spiritual influences that control the destiny of the unsaved.

Ephesians 2:2-3 speaks of evil influences at work in the world and thus in the unbeliever, which enslave everyone as children of wrath. Among those are the lust of the flesh and desires of the flesh and mind. John, in his first epistle, speaks of "all that is in the world, the lust of the flesh and the lust of the eyes and the boastful pride of life" (1 John 2:16). The use of "world" in Galatians 4:3 has led some commentators to favor this understanding. This would be true of Jew and Gentile alike, since all are sinners and are thus controlled by powers beyond their power to resist.

The phrase "elemental things" can be translated as "alphabet," as in Hebrews 5:12, and thus refer to Jewish laws and regulations. Colossians 2:8, 20 also seems to carry this meaning. If we accept that meaning here, then the elemental things would be elementary teachings regarding rules and regulations, by means of which people, both Jew and Gentile, each in their own way attempted to achieve salvation. For example, Gentiles would have been enslaved by prescriptions and ordinances related to appeasing their pagan deities. The Jews and proselytes to Judaism were looking to law-observance to find favor with God. This meaning of "elemental things" in verse 3 would certainly agree with the emphasis in verses 9-10.

I think it is highly likely that Paul may have both in view. It is true that all persons are enslaved by the world, sin, and their own desires. Equally true is that Jews were being held in bondage to a works-based religion by which they sought to earn righteousness before God. Whatever the case, these elemental things pale into insignificance with the fullness of time and the coming of Christ.

"The fullness of time" (v. 4) clearly recalls the emphasis on "the date set by the father" in verse 2. Verse 4 makes declarations about the sovereign timing of Christ's coming, His deity, and His humanity. "Fullness" means that the birth of Christ at its precise moment in history was God's eternal plan. Bible interpreters have pointed to the widespread use of the Greek language, the system of Roman roads, the relative political calm (*pax Romano),* the presence of synagogues, and the growing desire for real contact with God. While all these are relevant, the clear emphasis in verse 4 is on divine initiative and perfect timing.

"God sent forth His Son" assures us that God's Son existed from eternity past, a clear indication of his divinity. "Sent forth" means that the Son was sent on a divine mission. "Born of a woman" speaks to Christ's humanity; He assumed human nature (cf. John 1:14). Without surrendering His divinity, Christ became a human being who was not only born to affliction, pain, and trouble; He was also tempted in all points just as we are but without sin (cf. Heb. 4:15-16). Christ alone is the possessor of two natures—the divine and the human—united indissolubly in one person.

Paul added yet another phrase in Galatians 4:4—"born under the Law." Jesus was born a Jew and thus was under a personal obligation to obey its restrictions and demands. He was the only person to satisfy its demand for perfect obedience (cf. Gal. 3:10). For that reason, Christ alone could vicariously bear the law's penalty for all who fall short of perfect obedience.

Christ was born under the law "so that He might redeem those who were under the Law" (v. 5) and enable them to be adopted as sons. This verse expresses the same thought as 3:13, and the use of "we" indicates that Jews and Gentiles were both "under the law." We are all subject to it, for it expresses the righteousness of God, and we are all unable to carry it out through perfect obedience.

But there is more! We are not only delivered from the curse our disobedience brings; we are crowned with the greatest blessing possible—"that we might receive the adoption as sons." Paul's use of adoption imagery, rather than new birth, emphasizes the gracious selection by the Father. Then, as now, adoption bestows a new name, a new legal standing, and a new family relationship.

However, our adoption by the Father provides even more: "Because you are sons, God has sent forth the Spirit of His Son into our hearts, crying, 'Abba! Father!'" (4:6). *Abba* is the Aramaic informal word applied by a child to his or her father within the home. It is the very word Christ used to address His Father when He cried out to Him from the garden of Gethsemane concerning the cup He was about to drink on our behalf.

Verse 6 speaks of the proof of sonship; the Spirit's presence in the heart of the individual is an internal witness to the reality of all believers' family relationship (cf. Rom. 8:14-16). A person cannot be saved apart from the work of the Spirit, and every saved person receives the Spirit at the moment of salvation. Further, the Spirit works to incorporate us into the body of Christ (1 Cor. 12:13) by producing the fruit that enables us to live in community (cf. Rom. 12:9-21; 1 Cor. 13; Gal. 5:22–6:5; Eph. 4:1-6) and the gifts that enable us to contribute meaningfully to its mission and ministry.

All three members of the triune God are in cooperation in our redemption and consequent family relationship. The one true God sent forth the Son (Gal. 4:4) and the Spirit (v. 6). The Spirit is referred to as "the Spirit of His Son" because the Spirit proceeds from the Son (John 15:26) as well as from the Father. It is by the Spirit that Christ lives in our hearts (Eph. 3:16-17). The "heart" is the innermost self and thus controls the entire personality. The Holy Spirit not only brings us to Christ, providing for redemption; but He also permanently indwells us, giving us assurance and conforming us to the image of Christ.

Galatians 4:7 summarizes this entire section. Because of the influence of the Judaizers, the Galatians were behaving like slaves. Paul's assertion here is that they are no longer slaves; they are no longer under guardians awaiting the time set by the Father.

That time has come in Christ, and they are children and heirs. The word "heir" reminds us that sonship is not an achievement of merit but a marvelous act of grace; it is "through God." We inherit these wonderful blessings because of God's grace, not any works of merit on our part.

Would a Child Return to Slavery? (vv. 8-11)

Paul was concerned that persons who had found freedom in Christ would want to return to slavery. He called upon them to reflect on their lives before Christ. In the case of the Gentiles in Galatia, they were enslaved to gods that were false; they were not gods at all (v. 8; cf. Isa. 46:1). These so-called pagan deities had no power and could provide neither freedom nor joy. Paul, however, was not concerned that they would go back into bondage to heathenism; he was concerned that they were in danger of substituting the slavery of idolatry for the slavery of legalistic Judaism.

"But now" in verse 9 introduces the reminder that the Galatian believers had made a commitment that changed everything. They had come to know God. "To know" in the Bible is far deeper than intellectual knowledge; the term is used to speak of the intimate relationship between husband and wife. Paul quickly added a phrase that reminded them that God always takes the initiative in seeking humankind—"rather to be known by God." They had not accidentally groped their way to God; He had taken the costly initiative to know them by sending His Son into the world.

With God's love in view, how could the Galatians contemplate turning back to slavery? In their pagan past they were enslaved to false teachings of pagan priests. Having escaped one form of slavery, would they intentionally return to slavery, this time to Jewish regulations? The reference to "days and months and seasons and years" in verse 10 indicates they were already keeping some of the special times of the Jewish religious calendar, weekly Sabbaths and festivals such as Passover, Pentecost, and Tabernacles. Paul wanted them to understand that religious observances of any kind count nothing toward salvation.

We can hear the genuine angst in Paul's statement, "I fear for you" (v. 11). He feared that the Galatians' flight to legalism amounted to a rejection of the gospel they had joyfully professed. To use these verses to suggest Paul believed that the Galatians, or anyone else for that matter, could lose their salvation is misplaced. His tearful appeal indicates that he was working to win them back and was confident that their present failing was not final. The purpose of verse 11 is the same as that of the entire epistle—to rouse them to repent and return to the simple gospel that led to their salvation.

Where Is Your Sense of Blessing (vv. 12-16)?

Notice that Paul's strong reproof is now followed by a tender but urgent appeal: "I beg of you, brethren" (v. 12). Paul had once been a Jew bound by the law, trying futilely to earn God's favor through rigorous obedience. In Christ he was set free from the bondage of attempting to achieve righteousness through the law (cf. Phil. 3:7-11). He became like them in the sense that all humanity stands condemned because of sin and cannot claim to any self-righteous works for salvation.

Thus Paul appealed to the Galatian believers that they become like him—free from all legal observances. Ironically, the Galatians were moving toward the legalism Paul had abandoned gladly. His rather abrupt statement, "You have done me no wrong," may mean simply that he held no grudge against them despite their present deviation from his teaching. It may also be a subtle introduction to the following reminder on the kind manner in which the Galatians treated him when he first arrived.

Paul then reminded them that when he first arrived to preach the gospel they had received him as a messenger of God, as if Jesus Himself were speaking to them, despite Paul's physical infirmity (Gal. 4:13-14; cf. Acts 13:14–14:23). Paul calls this a bodily illness, such that it could have given rise to contempt. Luke referred to a physical issue (Acts 13:50; 14:5-6, 19), and Paul mentioned it to Timothy in his final letter (2 Tim. 3:10-11). There have been numerous suggestions as to the nature of his issue, such as epilepsy, eye trouble, and malaria, but it is unlikely we will ever resolve that question. The Galatians would have understood the reference clearly, which reminded them of the joy his visit brought them as they first heard the gospel.

The Galatians had experienced a season of thrilling discovery and had felt deeply blessed. So Paul questioned, "Where then is that sense of blessing you had?" (Gal. 4:15). The reference to their willingness to pluck out their eyes for him has caused some to conclude that Paul's illness was an eye disease. That seems unlikely, since an eye disease would have hardly caused someone to despise or loathe him. To tear out the eyes and give them to someone else is to give up one's most precious possession (cf. Deut. 32:10).

So what happened to their blessing? What clouded their relationship with Paul and caused some of them to regard him as an enemy? The simple answer is this: "the truth" (Gal. 4:16). The Galatians had welcomed the truth when they responded to Paul's message, but the influence of the Judaizers was causing some of them to reevaluate his message and to view him as an enemy. If

Paul was telling the truth, then simple logic indicates that those who troubled them were not.

Laboring until Christ Is Formed in You (vv. 17-20)

Paul questioned the motives of the Judaizers. Like all false teachers, the Judaizers wanted to make their converts dependent upon them. Their motive was not to develop spiritually mature followers of Christ but to make persons utterly dependent on them. The Judaizers were eagerly seeking the Galatians, but their motivation was not commendable. The Judaizers wanted to exclude the Galatians from all outside influence but their own (v. 17); and, in particular, they wanted to isolate them from any influence from Paul or his companions. Persons who try to live their Christian life by human directives and principles become dependent on the whims of their teachers.

Paul wanted them to seek him, but only in the right manner and for the right purposes. When Paul was present with them, the Galatians had shown great zeal for him, and he could only wish that zeal would remain even though he was no longer present (v. 18). Paul desired that he could be with them at present and that they would respond to his instructions to such a degree that he could change his tone (v. 20).

Whether absent or present, Paul's overarching goal was that Christ would be formed in the Galatian believers. Notice the use of the affectionate "my children" in verse 19. Unlike the Galatians, Paul's affection had not cooled. He was their father in the faith (cf. 1 Cor. 4:15); but in his present role he felt the pangs of a mother giving birth. The word "again" indicates he had gone through the labor pains once to give them new birth, and now he was laboring with them again.

Paul used the image of the development of a fetus into an infant to illustrate the formation of Christ in the life of the Galatians. "Christ is formed in you" (v. 19) means that the believer's inner being is fully surrendered to Christ (cf. Eph. 3:16-17). This is the work of the Spirit who changes us from glory to glory into his image (cf. 2 Cor. 3:17-18).

For Memory and Meditation

"But when the fullness of the time came, God sent forth His Son, born of a woman, born under the Law, so that He might redeem those who were under the Law, that we might receive the adoption as sons." (Gal. 4:4-5)

The Freedom to Pray

"Today, I joyfully call You "Daddy, my Father." I celebrate that I am no longer a slave to my passions and desires but have been set free; I am a child and an heir. Give me courage and strength to live in freedom as a child of the King."

Chapter 8

Children of Promise

Galatians 4:21-31

When I was pastor at First Baptist Norfolk, Mike and his wife, Kathy, worked with our young people. They were an amazing couple and were passionate about discipling youth. They simply loved children and treated the youth of the church like they would their own children. Sadly, Mike and Kathy had not been able to have any children of their own. From a medical standpoint it appeared that none would be in their future. But the Lord intervened, and Michael was born. Everyone was thrilled, especially Mike and Kathy. He was their miracle child, a child of promise.

Paul declared that everyone who belongs to Christ is a true descendant of Abraham and therefore an heir according to promise (3:29). He then set forth the privileges of sonship, which have been made available through Christ (4:1-20), and wondered aloud why any child would desire to be enslaved all over again. He continued to plead with those who were tempted to submit to the law to consider what the law itself teaches (v. 21).

The Two Sons of Abraham (vv. 21-23)

Paul began with a rhetorical question, causing the Galatian believers to think about the profound implications of coming under the law (v. 21). His argumentation may seem a bit forced to us, but it is typical of rabbinic exegesis of the time. We can assume that the Galatians had become fascinated by rabbinic exegesis from the Judaizers, and therefore Paul made his argument on territory familiar to them. He used allegorical interpretation in its most favorable sense by setting forth the spiritual meaning behind a familiar Old Testament story.

Sarah is described as representing freedom-loving people who live by faith. Her son was the son of promise. Hagar and her son represent those who were spiritually enslaved, attempting to live by the law. The Judaizers, and Galatians who were listening to them, wanted to make the case for the necessity of keeping the Mosaic law; and yet they were guilty of not listening to the law. In this case, Paul used the term *law* in a wider sense to mean the entire Pentateuch.

Based on our understanding that the destination of the letter was South Galatia, we can surmise that a large part of the congregation would have been from a Jewish background or a proselyte (Gentile who has converted to Judaism). They would have been offended by the implied suggestion that they did not bother to listen to the law.

"It is written" (v. 22) is a time-honored formula for beginning a quotation and is often used to introduce a pivotal text to cement an argument. Note that in discussing the law, Paul used a story from Abraham and not Moses, the human instrument through whom the law was given. We tend to overlook that when Jews refer to the law, they include Genesis as well as Leviticus and Deuteronomy. The *Torah*, the first five books of the Old Testament, was the instruction of God to his people. Historical events, understood as the saving acts of God, were equally as important as those that contained legislation. The Judaizers had placed more emphasis on the ritual aspect of the law and had conveniently ignored the larger story.

Paul mentioned Abraham's two sons but called neither by name, because his purpose was to show that one represents law, flesh, and slavery, while the other represents promise and freedom. Abraham had more than two sons, but these two are the only ones important to the point Paul was making from the Old Testament narrative. There was much Jewish interest in the story of Sarah and Hagar and their two sons, Isaac and Ishmael. Paul therefore employed a familiar story to make his case.

When Sarah was unable physically to bear a child, she decided to provide one through Hagar, her Egyptian slave (Gen. 16:1-4). This practice seems to have been socially acceptable at that time in history (see Gen. 30:3-13). "Born according to the flesh" (Gal. 4:23) may simply mean according to ordinary events or normal human processes without any miracle being involved and no promise of God. Yet, in the original story, the birth of Ishmael was not only a physical act but also one based on sinful deliberation. Abraham and Sarah did not wait for God's promise; they took matters into their own hands. Thus, Ishmael's birth represented a reliance on human planning rather than faith in divine promise.

Paul's spiritual lesson should be obvious to everyone. The birth of Ishmael, which relied only on the flesh, is like those who seek righteousness with God based on legal works. The birth of Isaac through promise is like those who know they must obtain favor with God by faith alone in Christ alone. Ishmael is representative of those who have experienced natural birth and not spiritual birth. He remains a slave, since he was born of a bondwoman. Isaac was born of a free woman through promise, and thus he is a symbol of all who are Spirit-born.

The Two Covenants (vv. 24-27)

Verse 24 clarifies that Paul was using typical allegorical language as he interpreted these two women as representative of the two covenants. The use of allegory in no way implies that Paul doubted the historical facts concerning this narrative; he simply wanted to draw out the deeper spiritual implications from the events. Since God is changeless, and since the spiritual principles derived from the events are changeless, this is no arbitrary interpretation. The Galatians must hear and respond to the truths contained in Scripture.

Notice the large number of opposites Paul used—bondwoman and free woman; flesh and promise; freedom and slavery; and present Jerusalem and Jerusalem above. All these contrasting pairs point to the two possible attitudes toward God—faith and works.

The Jews were proud to be called children of the covenant. Paul insisted they were children of a covenant made on Mount Sinai and not of the one made with Abraham. Jews would never have made this connection between Hagar's descendants and the law from Sinai, but the connection is works of the flesh versus faith in God's promises. So Paul gave to this Old Testament narrative an allegorical meaning that most Jews would meet with grim resistance. Attempting to achieve righteousness by the law brings a person into hopeless bondage and thus corresponds to the children of a bondwoman. This was a bitter pill to swallow because Jews prided themselves on being Isaac's offspring, not an Ishmaelite, the despised desert-dwellers of the Negev.

Paul used the term "present Jerusalem" in verse 25 to describe the rule-bound Judaism of the first century. Having linked Hagar and Mount Sinai, Paul again linked law and slavery. It is likely that those we refer to as Judaizers claimed to have some authority from the church at Jerusalem. Thus, Paul was not only saying that Jews who rejected Christ as Messiah were in bondage; those who appeared to be Christian in name but continued to rely on works of the law for salvation were still in bondage as well. All who trust in works of the flesh to obtain righteousness are children of Hagar and slaves.

Paul then spoke of the Jerusalem above, or the heavenly Jerusalem, as being the mother of true believers (v. 26). The concept of a new Jerusalem was familiar to Jews, based on the Old Testament. This was especially true when the old, familiar city had been destroyed. Passages such as Isaiah 62 and Ezekiel 48 made it easy to speak of an ideal Jerusalem, which already existed in heaven. In the Old Testament, Jerusalem could stand for the whole nation; and thus Paul was not simply talking about a city with the temple at its heart, but the whole nation of Israel.

The phrase "our mother" continues the imagery of motherhood that has permeated this section. To be children of the Jerusalem above means that we have already entered this eschatological age of fulfillment through faith in God's Messiah. The church constituted of all true believers, Jew and Gentile, is already being gathered. This same idea is articulated in Revelation 3:12; 21:2, 10. Though we still dwell on earth, heaven is our true home, and our lives are governed from heaven according to heavenly standards (cf. Phil. 3:20). The heavenly blessings the exalted Lord lavishes on His church are to enable us to advance His kingdom on earth, producing conditions on earth, which in some measure reflect those perfected in heaven (see Eph. 1). That is why believers pray for God's will to be done and His kingdom to come on earth as it is in heaven (Matt. 6:10).

The familiar quotation in verse 27 from Isaiah 54:1 is appropriate for many reasons. In the original context the prophet used the image of a barren woman to describe the glorious rebuilding of Israel after the Babylonian exile. For Paul, the barren woman represented Sarah, who had a child of divine promise late in life. Through the birth of Isaac and his descendants, Sarah would become the mother of more children than Hagar ("the one who has a husband"). Paul assured the small band of struggling believers of his day that they had a fruitful and glorious future.

You Are Children of Promise (4:28-31)

Paul again used the intimate address "brethren" twice (vv. 28, 31) as he concluded the allegory with the confident affirmation, "we are not children of a bondwoman, but of the free woman." He began by connecting the Galatians with Isaac and insisting that they were "children of promise." The comparison to Isaac assured them that they had spiritual life through God's promises to Abraham that Gentiles would be justified by faith (3:8). Being Jew or Gentile makes no difference; if Jerusalem above was their mother, then all were brothers and sisters in Christ.

Perhaps Paul anticipated that some might ask why they were being persecuted if Paul's ministry and their conversion was God's work. Paul again looked to the Old Testament narrative and commented that from the beginning Ishmael persecuted Isaac (see Gen. 21:8-9). For that reason, the Galatians should not be surprised that they faced persecution now. Beyond that, this is the inevitable reaction of all natural religions to all supernatural religion.

Paul again turned to Scripture to prove his case related to the priority of the true children of the free woman. The quotation in verse 30 from Genesis 21:10 speaks of the incident when Sarah asked Abraham to cast out Hagar and her son after Ishmael harassed Isaac. This verse indicates that Ishmael could not inherit along with Isaac. Paul quoted this passage to persuade the Galatians to reject all legalistic practices as a means of right standing with God. This explains why all natural (works-related) religious systems will always come into conflict with Christianity.

"So then" (v. 31) connects the conclusion to the main argument. Since Ishmael's fate was so horrific, true brethren will follow Isaac since they are sons of the free woman. Thus, "brethren" addresses those who are true Christ-followers. We are children of the free woman and must cling to this freedom.

For Memory and Meditation

"So then, brethren, we are not children of a bondwoman, but of the free woman." (Gal. 4:31)

The Freedom to Pray

"Father, I am awed to know that like Isaac of old, I am a child of promise, and I am free in Christ. Help me to embrace my freedom daily."

Chapter 9

It Was for Freedom that Christ Set Us Free!

Galatians 5:1-15

Even as a child I understood that freedom was both precious and costly. My parents were patriots and taught my siblings and me to cherish the freedom we experience as citizens of the United States. We were told of the wars that had been fought and the lives that had been sacrificed to purchase the freedom we enjoy daily and frequently take for granted. As I grew up in our Baptist tradition, I soon came to understand how our forefathers fought for religious freedom in the founding and expansion of our country.

I wrote this book during the COVID-19 "stay-at-home" order. During the first several weeks of the lockdown, most people—motivated by fear of contracting the virus—cooperated fully with the guidelines for gathering in large numbers, whether at work or at worship. As time went on, people began to wonder whether, in the name of safety, we were giving up some of the freedoms guaranteed to us in the Bill of Rights. This conversation does raise the question of what would prompt someone to give up something as precious as freedom.

Paul was not dealing with a lockdown caused by a virus, but he was writing to early Christians who were in danger of trading their newfound freedom in Christ for a form of slavery. Many of the early Galatian believers had come from a pagan background and had been enslaved by their own sin nature and the forces at work in the world. They were not tempted to return to the tyranny of paganism, but they were being influenced by false teachers to bind themselves to Jewish regulations in an effort to achieve righteousness.

Stand Firm in Freedom (v. 1)

This verse is essentially a stand-alone paragraph that bridges the truths established in the first four chapters to the practical application in chapters 5 and 6. The concept of Christian freedom is the theme of the first section, evidenced by the repetition of the word "freedom" in verses 1 and 13. The repetition created by "freedom" and "free" in the phrase "for freedom that Christ set us free" is a Semitic device intended to underline and reiterate the idea. We could paraphrase it thus: "It is ludicrous to think that Christ set us free merely to imprison us again."

For Paul, freedom includes deliverance from God's wrath and the penalty and power of sin. We are delivered from the penalty of sin because we no longer suffer the condemnation of the curse of the law (3:13). We are freed from the power of sin because we are now led by the Spirit and are no longer under the law (5:18). Thus, Paul's clear focus in this section is on freedom from the curse that the law places on the sinner who has been working unsuccessfully to achieve righteousness through it.

Freedom is more than mere deliverance; it is a positive liberation under which the believer walks and lives in and by the Spirit (v. 25), enabling him or her to produce the fruit of the Spirit and fulfill the law of Christ (6:2). An individual who is free no longer acts from legalistic desire to obey the law but serves God willingly empowered by the Spirit.

"Keep standing firm" in 5:1 translates a present active imperative, meaning first that it is a command and not a suggestion.

Second, the present tense indicates that the action that is commanded is continual and habitual. Further, the imagery is that of a soldier on a field (Eph. 6:13-14). For the Galatians to stand firm, they must reject the yoke of slavery. In Peter's speech before the Jerusalem Council, defending the mission to the Gentiles, he referred to the law in terms of an unbearable yoke (Acts 15:10). "Yoke" is the same word Jesus used in Matthew 11:29-30 to refer to the "easy" yoke of following Him. The Galatians were in danger of exchanging the yoke of pagan superstition for the yoke of Jewish regulations.

Waiting for the Hope of Righteousness (vv. 2-6)

Remember that Paul began his appeal in chapters 1 and 2 with a reminder of history, both his and theirs. In chapters 3 and 4 he argued from Scripture, establishing that the teaching of the Judaizers was contradicted by the Torah they claimed to teach and believe. In the last two chapters of Galatians Paul will move to the practical argument of the moral change brought about by the gospel. Persons in Christ experience a freedom and exhibit behavior that is not produced by the restraints of Jewish law.

The stately address in verse 2, "Behold I, Paul," in conjunction with the word "testify" in verse 3, gives this section the character of a declaration under oath and thus reminded the Galatian believers of his apostolic authority. Since some of the Galatians were already yielding to the temptation to observe various Jewish festivals (4:10), Paul feared they might also yield in the matter of circumcision. Paul, who was justifiably proud of his Jewish background and traditions (Phil. 3:4-6), declared circumcision to be of no value in obtaining a right standing with God.

The verb tenses are worthy of note. "If you receive circumcision" implies that the practice was being considered by some in

Galatia but had not yet taken place. It would also suggest that Paul did not condemn Jewish Christians who were already circumcised. In 1 Corinthians 7:17-20 Paul provides a more detailed teaching on the issue of circumcision and one's conversion, concluding that "circumcision is nothing, and uncircumcision is nothing" (v. 20). Possibly some of the Judaizers had been accusing Paul of condemning Jewish Christians who were already circumcised or had suggested that they should not have their own children circumcised (cf. Acts 21:21).

Paul condemned the teaching that circumcision, or any other act of human effort, was necessary for salvation. He warned, in very strong language, that to choose circumcision was to negate all the benefits Christ offers. To submit to circumcision in the hope that it was necessary for salvation would be to add works to faith and would demonstrate that the Galatians had not understood the simple gospel nor trusted Christ as Savior. The gospel is grace alone by faith alone, and any attempt to supplement it with works is to misunderstand and distort it.

The use of "testify" in Galatians 5:3 continues the solemn and authoritative tone of this section. Paul used this same word in Acts 20:26 and 26:22 to defend his actions before the Ephesian elders and Agrippa. "Every man" means each member individually and personally. Any person who received circumcision demonstrated that he was trusting in the law (works religion) for salvation. To accept circumcision as necessary for salvation was to accept the entire law as being necessary. The law is a unit whose commands are inextricably linked together (James 2:1). Once the choice to earn righteousness by the law is made, the individual must follow that path to the very end, which means obedience to the whole law. Paul had already shown that this path was a dead end (Gal. 3:10).

If the Galatians were to accept circumcision as necessary for salvation, it would mean that they did not view Christ's death as sufficient and were thus attempting to supplement the work that He completed on the cross. In this sense, they severed themselves from Christ as the only means of salvation (5:4). The word *severed* means to abolish a relationship (cf. Rom. 7:2). They would be choosing law-righteousness over a personal relationship with Christ.

The phrase "fallen from grace" further explains the dilemma facing the Galatians. To choose the law would mean they had abandoned the realm where grace is operative and had chosen works of righteousness. The context is clear that a fall from the realm of grace is a choice in favor of legalism as the way to God. Grace and works are mutually exclusive as it relates to salvation.

Some persons have used the phrase "fallen from grace" as a description of a Christian who has lapsed into sin and is in danger of losing salvation. Such a distorted understanding of this text comes from ignoring the full context. Throughout this letter, and particularly this section, Paul contrasted two paths to salvation—works and grace. A person who attempts to keep the law in order to gain salvation abandons the true way to God, which is faith in Christ.

I once had a seminary professor who enjoyed alliteration. He would often say, "The faith that fizzles before the finish had a flaw from the first." That simple alliteration explains Paul's concern. If the Galatians were to choose circumcision and the entire legal system as their hope for salvation, it would indicate that their understanding of the gospel was defective from the beginning, and Paul's labor there would have been in vain.

Paul used "we" in verse 5 to include himself and to assure his readers of his confidence that they were not among those who had chosen the realm of the law over that of grace. They were included in those who "through the Spirit, by faith are waiting for the hope of righteousness." "Through the Spirit" indicates that conviction of sin and salvation are initiated by the Holy Spirit. "By faith" is a human's necessary response. The tension between God's sovereign activity in salvation and a human's necessary response is maintained throughout Scripture. "Through the Spirit, by faith" as the only means of salvation distinguishes Christianity from every other world religion.

The use of "hope" in this verse and throughout Paul's writings does not suggest any element of doubt as it often does in our conversation. Romans 5:1-5 is an excellent commentary on the meaning of biblical hope. Notice that verse 5 of the Romans passage connects the assurance of hope with the ministry of the Holy Spirit: "And hope does not disappoint, because the love of God has been poured out within our hearts through the Holy Spirit who was given to us."

Those who look to the law (works) for salvation can never have assurance of a right standing before God, but those who are born again by the Spirit wait eagerly and confidently for the hope of righteousness. "Righteousness" means right standing before God, which will be revealed fully at the coming of Christ when all believers will be completely transformed into righteousness.

Galatians 5:6 serves as a summary statement. Notice that the argument is not one-sided. Paul would not allow a Gentile believer to boast of his uncircumcised condition; regarding salvation it has no meaning. The real evidence of salvation is not circumcision, but faith that operates through love. Works of love flow out of authentic faith and give evidence of its genuine character. This verse and the remainder of this letter are clear evidence that Paul and James were in complete agreement that works flow naturally from authentic faith (James 2:22). Perhaps you have heard the saying, "Works are fruit and not root."

I Have Confidence in You (vv. 7-12)

While Paul's goal in this section was to express confidence in the Galatians, he also wanted to point out the devious and destructive work of the false teachers. He employed several different words to describe their work: "hindered" (v. 7); "persuasion" (v. 8); "disturbing" (v. 10); and "troubling" (v. 12).

Paul began with a metaphor from the running track that dominated the Greek athletic world. The runner gets off to a great start and then is hindered by another runner who cuts in on him or her and inhibits further progress. The question, "who hindered you?" in verse 7 is not a request for information but a question requiring them to consider their lack of progress in obeying the truth. "Truth" refers to God's special revelation as embodied in the gospel proclaimed by Paul and his fellow workers.

The persuasion to abandon obedience to the gospel did not come from God through the Holy Spirit. Had the Galatian believers lost the ability to distinguish the work of the Holy Spirit from human treacherous persuasion?

Perhaps they underestimated the danger of listening to the persuasive arguments of the Judaizers. So Paul employed a well-known proverb, "A little leaven leavens the whole lump of dough" (v. 9). "Leaven" or "yeast" is used frequently in the Gospels as a symbol of pervasive evil (cf. Matt. 13:33). During the Feast of Unleavened Bread, the removal of leaven from the house was a solemn ritual for Jews and a symbol of putting away sin (cf. 1 Cor. 5:7-8). These false teachers may have been few, but their potential for negative impact was great.

Chapter 9

Throughout the letter Paul consistently expressed deep concern, along with his conviction that this letter would have its desired effect (cf. Gal. 3:4; 4:6-7). The phrase "in the Lord" (v. 10) indicates that Paul had this confidence from the Lord (cf. Phil. 2:6). He was certain the Galatians would adopt no other view than the one he shared with them, leading to their conversion. Paul was also certain that "the one who is disturbing you" would bear God's judgment. The phrase "whoever he is" may not mean that Paul did not know his identity but may be an ironic reference to his lack of status.

Paul's self-defense in verse 11 seems a bit abrupt and may suggest that he was aware that his opponents had accused him of being inconsistent in the matter of circumcision. Their accusation may have been because Paul had allowed Timothy to be circumcised. Paul permitted Timothy, a person of mixed parentage, to be circumcised to enable him to be a more effective missionary among the Jews. Never was there any thought that circumcision was necessary for his salvation. In accepting circumcision for Timothy and opposing it for the Galatians, Paul was consistent in promoting the essence of the gospel.

Further, the fact that Paul was being persecuted by the Judaizers proved that he was not preaching a message of accommodation. Paul reminded them that the offensive nature of the cross would disappear if he advocated circumcision as a requirement for salvation. The cross reminds all of us of our utter helplessness and dependence on divine grace. The cross is a scandal to the Jews and to everyone who advocates a works-based righteousness.

Verse 12 concludes this section with a rather startling expression. Some translations use the phrase "cut off" rather than "mutilate." Some commentators take the meaning "cut off" to mean that Paul wanted the Judaizers to cut themselves off from the church.

The more likely meaning, which most translations echo, indicate that Paul was suggesting that the agitators advocating circumcision should go all the way and make eunuchs of themselves through castration. Some commentators think Paul may have been setting circumcision in its true light as one of many ritual cuttings practiced in the ancient world. Paul was not seriously suggesting castration; he was using irony to shock the Galatians into realizing that, robbed of all its spiritual significance, circumcision had simply become bodily mutilation.

This bold image may seem a bit shocking to our ears, but it is not intended to be crude. We should be reminded what Jesus said about anyone who causes a little one to stumble (Matt. 18:6). Doctrinal integrity was and is an issue of eternal importance.

Through Love Serve One Another (vv. 13-15)

Paul then returned to the theme of freedom with which he began the chapter (5:1). It may be that the Judaizers were concerned that Paul's rejection of the law as necessary for salvation could lead to lawless behavior. It is also likely that some of the Galatians had used freedom as a pretext for selfish and sinful behavior. Christian freedom is not freedom to sin, but rather freedom from sin and freedom to serve. The abuse of Christian freedom as an excuse for sinful and selfish behavior is seen in several Pauline letters (cf. Rom. 6:1).

Freedom, unrestrained, provides an opportunity for the flesh to express itself. Paul frequently used "flesh" in apposition to "spirit." Mortal humankind is flesh, and flesh is corruptible in nature. If this corruption is not impeded by the power of the indwelling Holy Spirit, it produces the works of the flesh such as those articulated in verses 19-22. While Paul warned against bondage to the law in a negative sense, he promoted bondage of love to one another.

The true aspiration of freedom is "through love serve one another" (v. 13). Our service is modeled after one who laid aside his rights of being equal to God and took on the form of a servant (Phil. 2:7) and who later laid aside His garments and washed the feet of His disciples on the eve of His crucifixion (John 13:3-20). The verb translated "serve one another" is present tense, indicating that it is an ongoing action. To reinforce his call to loving service, in verse 15 Paul quoted Leviticus 19:18. Paul wanted to show that loving action is obedience to the law.

The opposite of serving one another is biting and devouring one another. The picture is that of a wild pack of animals nipping and biting one another until they are all devoured. When all is said and done, nothing will remain. These are good warnings for Christians of every generation.

For Memory and Meditation

"For you were called to freedom, brethren; only do not turn your freedom into an opportunity for the flesh, but through love serve one another." (Gal. 5:13)

The Freedom to Pray

"Father, forgive me when I see my freedom as a matter of personal pride that leads again to sin. Help me to resist pride by putting others before myself in true service."

Chapter 10

The Fruit of the Spirit

Galatians 5:16-24

One of the first issues new believers face is the stark and brutal reality that they still struggle with the issue of sin. In the first blush of conversion the sense of forgiveness of sin is so powerful that we assume we will never again struggle with evil desires and thoughts. Then reality sets in! Our battle with the flesh intensifies, and our sense of shame grows. We may wonder if we have truly been born again.

If you can identify, you may find some comfort in knowing that the great apostle Paul dealt with the same struggle between the desires of the flesh and the ministry of the Spirit: "I find then the principle that evil is present in me, the one who wants to do good. For I joyfully concur with the law of God in the inner man, but I see a different law in the members of my body, waging war against the law of my mind and making me a prisoner of the law of sin which is in my members" (Rom. 7:21-23). He then celebrated the liberation that came through Christ who sets us free from the law of sin and death: "Thanks be to God through Jesus Christ our Lord!" (v. 25). This freedom from sin and victory over the flesh continues for those who set their minds on the Spirit and walk in His power.

In Galatians 5:16-24 Paul calls on the Galatians to walk by the Spirit that they might experience freedom from the deeds of the flesh. He provides a lengthy list of deeds of the flesh, which are then contrasted with the fruit produced by the Spirit. This list is not intended to be comprehensive, but many of the deeds of the flesh listed here were related specifically to matters that were germane to new believers in Galatia.

Flesh and Spirit at War (vv. 16-18)

As we begin our study of these verses, it is important to remember the immediate context. In verse 13 Paul warned the Galatians about the danger of allowing their newfound freedom from the legalism prescribed by the Judaizers to become an opportunity for the flesh. In other words, freedom from the law does not mean that we are free to indulge the desires of the flesh. True freedom is expressed as believers serve one another through love. Fleshly behavior in community is destructive, as is clearly expressed by the phrase "bite and devour one another" (v. 15).

The phrase "but I say" in verse 16 introduces a contrast to behavior that is destructive to the individual and the faith community. The use of "walk" was a common expression to refer to the living of one's life. "Spirit" is a reference to the Holy Spirit, who is given to all believers at the time of conversion. In 1 Corinthians 12:3 Paul tells us that no one can utter the confession "Jesus is Lord" except by the Holy Spirit. Similarly, in Romans 8:9 he declared, "If anyone does not have the Spirit of Christ, he does not belong to Him." In verse 11 he then affirmed that the Spirit not only effects conversion but indwells those who are in Christ.

The command to "walk by the Spirit" in Galatians 5:16 is in the present tense, indicating the continuous need for the Spirit's power to enable holy living. When we follow the Spirit's directions and promptings, we are not dominated by "the desire of the flesh." "Flesh" refers to human nature, the seat of fleshly desires. Paul depicted the ferocious and unrelenting struggle between Spirit and flesh, a conflict described more completely in Romans 7:15-23.

The indwelling Spirit and the old nature are "in opposition to one another" with the result that we cannot, in our own strength, do the things we desire to do (Gal. 5:17).

Paul was describing the battle in the believer's heart when he or she does not walk in the Spirit. The unsaved person does not experience this struggle, for he or she follows natural inclinations. It is true that from time to time these persons may be pierced in their conscience about their evil behavior, but they rarely do battle. Legalists, such as those confusing the Galatians, struggle with the flesh but cannot achieve victory because they are unwilling to accept grace. Believers, while still engaged in this earthly journey, often experience agonizing conflict, but in principle have already gained victory as the presence of the Holy Spirit testifies. Victory can be realized as we surrender to the Spirit's control.

Being led by the Spirit does not mean that the believer is passive; it involves active surrender and dependence on God's power. Paul used words such as "walk" (v. 16), "led" (v. 18), and "live" (v. 25) to describe the necessary response of the believer.

Paul contrasted being "led by the Spirit" with being "under the law" (v. 18). As we have seen thus far in Galatians, the law means defeat, bondage, and curse, because it is impotent to save and deliver from sin. The law stimulates sin because the flesh refuses to submit to it (cf. Rom. 8:3, 7). The solution to the believer's problem with the flesh is not law but Spirit.

Being led by the Spirit is for all believers, at all times—not for spiritual super-heroes at critical moments. We sometimes hear people talking about having a higher nature and a lower one in conflict. They then imply that by sheer effort we can determine which nature wins. The winning formula is not greater effort but total surrender to the Holy Spirit's leading.

Chapter 10

The Holy Spirit is a distinct person of the Trinity who indwells the believer and produces fruit in and through one's life. Sometimes the process of following the Spirit is spoken of as ongoing sanctification, whereby the believer becomes more like Christ. He enables us in an ongoing and growing manner to defeat the power of indwelling sin and to obey God's word cheerfully.

The Deeds of the Flesh (vv. 19-21)

In verse 19 Paul calls deeds of the flesh "evident" because they are plainly observable. They include both inward attitudes and outward actions. These "deeds" arise from a corrupt human nature, which is self-centered and hostile toward God. Similar lists can be found in Jesus's teaching (Mark 7:21-22), in other Pauline letters (Rom. 1:24-32; 1 Cor. 6:9-10; Eph. 5:3-4; 1 Tim. 1:9-10), and even in the writing of pagan moralists. Some pagan moralists, however, viewed them with horror and as contrary to humanity's true nature. Scripture views them as the natural actions of fallen human nature.

Various commentators have pointed out that the list in 5:19-21 appears to place the fifteen "deeds of the flesh" into categories. The first three are sexual sins; the next two deal with false worship; eight deal with broken personal relationships; and the final two with intemperance. If Paul intended for the reader to draw any conclusion from this categorization of the deeds of the flesh, perhaps it is the predominance of those pertaining to personal relationships. While we often make much of sexual sins and those related to drunkenness (and we should), we are prone to excuse those sins that hinder interpersonal relationships and consequently destroy families and churches.

"Immorality" is a general word, used broadly for impure sexual relationships of any kind. "Impurity" referred originally to ceremonial impurity; but it was later used in reference to moral impurity, which hindered fellowship with God (cf. 1 Th. 4:7). Impurity is not just a matter of outward deeds but also speaks of thoughts and desires of the heart. "Sensuality" emphasizes the lack of self-control. Sexual immorality was commonplace in the ancient world and was often connected to pagan worship. Clearly Paul had to fight such sins in Gentile churches, which may have fed the Judaizers' desire to emphasize the need for the law. One thing is certain—Christianity's call for sexual purity was as radical an idea then as it is today.

"Idolatry," at its base level, is the worship of anything or anyone rather than the one true God. For example, in Colossians 3:5 Paul denounces greed, the worship of money, as a form of idolatry. Sorcery and witchcraft were widespread in the first century. Acts 19:19 tells us that the books related to magical practices that were burned in Ephesus were worth fifty thousand pieces of silver. The term translated "sorcery" in Galatians 5:19 is from the Greek *pharmakeia*, from which we get the English word "pharmacy." Drugs were, and still are, often related to idolatrous worship, including witchcraft.

The third grouping of sins is the largest and refers to rivalry of the baser sort. They have their root in a loveless, selfish, and prideful disposition. Each one destroys trust, promotes hostility, and ruptures all community relationships. In light of 5:15, these were sins of particular severity in Galatia. "Enmities" (v. 20) are any mental attitudes that erect barriers and produce hostility between persons, races, and classes. "Strife" is discord and quarreling, created when people start to choose sides. "Jealousy" is self-interest that causes a person to resent the success and accomplishments of others. These two are also joined in Romans 13:13, because what may start as intense devotion to a leader or idea can degenerate into jealous infighting.

Chapter 10

How strife and jealousy would lead to "outbursts of anger" is easy to understand. This phrase refers to a fiery flash of rage that is passionate and temporary. "Disputes" and "dissensions" are often the result of self-seeking ambition that regards a person's own agenda to be paramount. The attitudes listed above will inevitably lead to "factions" or small groups that pridefully keep to themselves and promote their own agendas to the detriment of the larger community. "Envying" (v. 21) in the English comes from a Latin word that means "to look against" and thus means to look at another person with a hostile spirit because of what he or she is or has. These attitudes and sins manifest themselves in a congregation who does not walk by the Spirit.

Paul concluded this section with two sins related to intemperance. "Drunkenness" refers to the excessive consumption of alcohol. The Bible speaks of alcohol abuse as a sin and not just a disease. We can give the disease aspect of drug and alcohol addiction due concern without ignoring the responsibility of the individual who comes to that point. "Carousing" speaks of drinking parties or drunken orgies. It is possible that in the first century such parties were carried out in the public worship of pagan deities.

The phrase "and things like these" indicates that Paul did not intend this list to be comprehensive. This conclusion would be substantiated by comparing other similar lists in the Pauline letters. We can further conclude that many of those sins selected for inclusion were of special relevance to the new converts in Galatia. The mention of forewarning must refer to Paul's teaching while he was in Galatia. This suggests that Paul did a considerable amount of teaching (discipling) when persons originally responded to the gospel.

Not only did Paul warn the Galatian believers about sinful practices, he was clear "that those who practice such things will not inherit the kingdom of God." "Practice" speaks of the habitual continuation of deeds of the flesh. Such persons would, by these practices, demonstrate that they lack the indwelling of the Holy Spirit. It does not mean that someone who has committed one or more of these is in danger of losing salvation. If a person has been truly born again and indwelt by the Spirit, such behavior will lead to repentance. The phrase "inherit the kingdom of God" looks back to the discussion in chapters 3 and 4 about becoming an heir. The kingdom of God describes the rule of God in the present and future. Paul articulated clearly two complementary truths—no one can gain access to the kingdom through the practice of good deeds, but a person can demonstrate his or her lack of Kingdom access by habitual evil practices. If someone refuses to bid farewell to works of the flesh, he or she reveals the absence of the indwelling Spirit.

The Spontaneous and Organic Product of the Spirit (vv. 22-24)

Fruit is the natural and organic product of a healthy plant. Jesus used the image of organic fruit in His inaugural message in Matthew 7. He warned the listening crowd to beware of false prophets who could be identified by the fruit of their lives. He first noted that neither grapes nor figs could be gathered from thorn bushes or thistles (vv. 15-16). He said, "So every good tree bears good fruit, but the bad tree bears bad fruit. A good tree cannot produce bad fruit, nor can a bad tree produce good fruit" (vv. 17-18). The internal DNA of the tree determines the fruit that will appear on its branches. In the same way, the indwelling Spirit will naturally and spontaneously produce fruit that is consistent with the very character of Christ. Surrender to the Spirit is required on the part of the believer, not willpower or human effort.

Chapter 10

The word "fruit" in Galatians 5:22 is singular, indicating that the entire harvest of fruit is produced by the Holy Spirit. We are not free to choose among them as if we are selecting character traits from a buffet line. Fruit of the Spirit is the natural result of the Spirit-empowered life and therefore a clear indication of His presence.

Many commentators point out that the fruit can be grouped into three groups of three. The first three are the most basic inward qualities essential to Christian living. The second group contains those that are essential to interpersonal relationships, an issue that was critical to the divided church at Galatia. The final three focus on the believer in relationship to God's will (faithfulness), in relationship with others (gentleness), and in relationship to his or her inner self (self-control).

Heading the list is "love" *(agape)*, which is based on God's love and prompted Him to send Christ to die for sinners (John 3:16). Love was both modeled and prescribed by Christ (John 13:1, 34; 17:26). Paul placed it above faith and hope as being the necessary requisite for living in community and exercising the gifts (1 Cor. 13:13). Love involves the entire person; it engages the mind, will, and emotions in such a manner that it leads to loving actions.

Where love abounds, joy is always present. Love fulfills the law (Rom. 13:10), which in turn causes delight. Joy is not like happiness, which depends on pleasant circumstances; joy enables believers to rejoice in the most trying of circumstances (1 Peter 1:8). "Peace" probably refers to a person's relationship with God and reflects the idea of wholeness. This serenity of heart will naturally be reflected in one's relationship with others, as the peace possessor becomes a peacemaker (cf. Matt. 5:9). Paul's mention of peace provides a natural link to the second group.

"Patience" is the fruit that enables us to endure both trying circumstances and trying people. It is an attitude of restraint at the heart of God's relationship with sinful humanity (2 Peter 3:15) and was modeled by His Son (1 Tim. 1:16). When we struggle with the fruit of patience, it is helpful to remember how patient God has been with us. Kindness is the concrete thoughtfulness Christians demonstrate to others based on how God has treated us (Eph. 4:32). Galatians 6:1 may indicate that Paul feared that the "orthodox" Galatians might respond negatively toward weaker brothers who had succumbed to the teaching of the Judaizers. We will look at this passage in the next chapter. "Goodness" is a generous spirit that develops from kindness and acts even when undeserved.

The final three begins with "faithfulness," which means trustworthiness, reliability, and fidelity. First of all, faithfulness toward God and His work is required (cf. 2 Tim. 2:2), and it will be reflected in all of one's actions and relationships. "Gentleness" in verse 23 is a word Christ used to describe Himself (Matt. 11:29). It describes the Christian who submits to the Spirit's control and a righteous way of life. Outside the New Testament this word was used to describe an animal that had been tamed to accept discipline and thus had become useful to its owner. "Self-control" requires personal restraint and thus the ability to keep one's passions and desires in check. To exercise this fruit, we must bring every thought captive to Christ (cf. 2 Cor. 10:5).

Paul concluded the listing with an unusual statement: "against such things there is no law." First, "such things" indicates that this list is not to be viewed as exhausting the work of the Spirit. The reference to law is particularly important in light of the emphasis by the Judaizers on the necessity of law-keeping. Paul affirmed that those persons who walk by the Spirit will fulfill the law, not through legalistic dictum, but from the inner being through the power of the Spirit. In truth, they will go beyond mere outward obedience to inner fulfillment of the very intent of the law. This would comply with Jesus's intensification of the law in His sermon on the mount (cf. Matt. 5:21-48).

In Galatians 2:20 Paul declared his co-crucifixion with Christ. In this context, the crucifixion of the flesh is the basis for producing a rich spiritual harvest that is manifested by the indwelling Spirit. Paul called on the Galatian believers to put into practice that which they already were in principle. To live in victory over "passions and desires," we must rely continually on the Spirit.

For Memory and Meditation

"But the fruit of the Spirit is love, joy, peace, patience, kindness, goodness, faithfulness, gentleness, self-control; against such things there is no law." (Gal. 5:22-23)

The Freedom to Pray

"Father, forgive me for too often depending on the flesh to control my behavior. Produce in me the fruit of Your Spirit, which gives perfect freedom."

Chapter 11

The Spirit in Community

Galatians 5:25–6:10

Through the years I have encountered numerous persons who claimed to be followers of Christ and who insisted that they had no need for the church. When I use the word *church* I am not referring to a specific denominational identity nor am I referring to the more nebulous "universal church"; I am using it in a more general sense of a local gathering of like-minded believers. In other words, these persons felt they did not need to fellowship with other believers to express their devotion to Christ. Some even commented that they feel closer to God in nature than they do when gathered with the church.

I love nature, and I do feel God's presence when I observe the wonder of His creation. But I have a special love for the church because it is the bride of Christ. When Peter first publicly declared, "You are the Christ, the Son of the living God," Jesus responded by declaring that upon this bedrock confession to His messianic identity, He would build His church. He further promised to give to it the keys of the kingdom, investing it with such power that the gates of Hades could not stand against it (Matt. 16:13-19). Luke began his second volume (Acts 1:1) by indicating that his first volume only contained what Jesus "began to do and teach." The clear implication is that Jesus continues to work through His church to advance His kingdom until He returns for His bride.

If you consult various commentaries on Galatians, you may notice that most include Galatians 5:25-26 with the discussion of fruit of the Spirit and begin a new section with 6:1. It is clear that these two sections are closely related since they both begin with the phrase "walk by the Spirit" (5:16) and "let us walk by the Spirit" (v. 25). However, the repetition of the phrase "let us" in 5:25, 26 and 6:9, 10 may indicate that Paul was turning his attention to the fruit of the Spirit as it relates to living in community.

The Ministry of the Spirit in Building Community (5:25-26)

"Live by the Spirit" means that our new life in Christ is directed and empowered by the Holy Spirit who brings us to Christ and, upon conversion, indwells us. The reception of the Holy Spirit is sometimes referred to as the baptism of the Holy Spirit. Some teach wrongly that the baptism of the Spirit is a separate event from salvation, as if God withholds His empowering presence until the believer adds some further act of commitment subsequent to salvation. Such an idea sounds like the argument of the Judaizers who insisted that Gentile believers had to add law-obedience to their original commitment.

Paul's writings teach clearly that "if anyone does not have the Spirit of Christ, he does not belong to Him" (Rom. 8:9). The indwelling Spirit gives life to our mortal bodies (v. 11). Those persons who are being led by the Spirit "are sons of God," enabled to "cry out 'Abba! Father!'" (vv. 14, 15). Romans 8:16 tells us that "the Spirit Himself testifies with our spirit that we are children of God." He "helps our weakness" by interceding for us "according to the will of God" (vv. 26-27). In 1 Corinthians 12 Paul tells us that the Spirit also distributes spiritual gifts that enable us to work for the common good and baptizes us into one body (vv. 7, 13). The fruit of the Spirit enables us to live and serve together in the body of Christ in its earthly imperfection.

The phrase in Galatians 5:25, "if we live by the Spirit," does not express doubt, and therefore we could accurately paraphrase, "Since we have new life by the Spirit, we must let the Spirit direct the course of our lives." To "walk by the Spirit" means that we constantly rely on the Spirit to put to death the sinful acts that characterized our old lives and produce the fruit indicative of His indwelling presence.

The actions indicated by verse 26— "boastful, challenging one another, envying one another"—remind us of the earlier warning in verse 15 about biting and devouring one another. Likely the actions mentioned in verse 26 are directed specifically to persons in Galatia. Perhaps those who had not fallen for the teaching of the Judaizers were now boasting of their spiritual strength. Paul was speaking specifically about pride and a know-it-all attitude that could easily lead to rivalry and envy. He used a Greek word that pictures challenges in athletic contests. In other words, fellow believers should not pick fights with one another. The Spirit-controlled life produces fruit that will have a definite effect in personal relationships.

Bear One Another's Burdens (6:1-5)

The Spirit does not simply empower us to avoid destructive behaviors that negatively impact community; He enables us to "bear one another's burdens" (v. 2). One specific way we build community is by restoring a person who "is caught in any trespass" (v. 1). The word *caught* suggests an element of unexpectedness. It is not so much that someone caught the Galatians in a sinful act, but rather that they were overtaken, or caught unexpectedly, by sinful behavior.

Some debate exists as to the meaning of the term "spiritual." A similar designation is used throughout 1 Corinthians to describe persons who hold an inflated opinion of themselves based on the possession of certain spiritual gifts. Neither that description nor situation seems to apply to the churches in Galatia. Some think the use here may be ironic, as if Paul is saying, "You who claim to be so spiritual can prove it by acting maturely in community." I think it is best to take it at face value. "You who are spiritual" refers to those persons walking by the Spirit.

Spirit-controlled Christians take no pleasure in another person's sin, but rather seek to restore them in a spirit of gentleness. It is noteworthy that "gentleness" is an aspect of the fruit of the Spirit mentioned above (5:23). Paul was not setting up an "elite spiritual task force" whose role it was to monitor the community for sin and set upon a "holier-than-thou" rescue mission. In 1 Thessalonians, the letter that follows this one in chronological order, Paul admonishes the brethren to "admonish the unruly, encourage the fainthearted, help the weak, be patient with everyone" (5:14). This is what it means to live in community as the body of Christ.

The word translated "restore" in Galatians 6:1 is the same word used in Matthew 4:21 for the mending of nets. The goal is to assist a brother or sister in his or her spiritual walk by helping to restore them to their former condition. The basic idea is that the spiritual person desires to help and not hinder. Paul warned that individuals must examine themselves so they will not be tempted. Spiritual pride is such a devious enemy; none of us can let down our guard, thinking sin will never catch us by surprise.

Paul commanded the Galatians to "bear one another's burdens" (v. 2), which would enable them to fulfill the law of Christ. The word translated "burden" here is a Greek word that signifies a heavy burden and would thus mean issues such as spiritual failure, persecution, or poverty. The Judaizers had been eager to convince the Galatians to keep the law of Moses, but Paul appealed to a higher way that would enable them to keep the law of Christ. The law of Christ is the principle of love for one another, which Jesus established as a new commandment (John 13:34).

That which makes us gentle and kind to others is a realistic view of ourselves. Spiritual overevaluation—"if anyone thinks he is something"—is dangerous and leads to self-deceit (Gal. 6:3). Paul was thinking of a person's poor spiritual state rather than his or her relative unimportance. He attacked the spirit of pride and overconfidence in one's own power, the self-righteousness revealed by the Judaizers throughout this letter. This is the only use of the verb translated "deceives himself." The noun version of the word is found in Titus 1:10 in regard to "those of the circumcision." Spiritual conceit can lead to intolerance of another's failure and to an unfounded belief that you are above such failure.

We are not to compare our spiritual accomplishments with those of others. When we make such comparisons, we are guilty of judging the labor of another believer (Gal. 6:4). Further, to make ourselves look good, we search for someone doing less than us. I cannot tell you how many times I have heard someone declare, "I do more than most" to justify that person's own lack of involvement. When a person compares him- or herself to God's standards, and there is obvious value, then he or she can boast about what God has accomplished through him or her.

Paul ended the section by talking about personal responsibility: "For each one will bear his own load" (v. 5). The declaration of individual responsibility does not contradict the demand to "bear one another's burdens" in verse 2. "Burdens" refers to a heavy or crushing weight, while the Greek word used in verse 5 was used to refer to the pack of a soldier. It indicates one's personal responsibilities, which must be borne alone. Heavy burdens are to be borne jointly in community, while each of us must shoulder our own load by doing our assigned task.

Sharing Good Things with Your Teacher (6:6)

Many of the Galatian believers were from a pagan background and were unaccustomed to providing financial support for religious teachers. The phrase translated "share all good things" clearly implies financial remuneration. Possibly Paul may have anticipated that some persons in Galatia might be tempted to use the thought of verse 5 to argue that teachers should bear their own load. Paul wanted them to understand clearly that those who serve in church vocations have a right to expect generous support from the people whom they serve.

Since Galatians is Paul's earliest letter, and therefore one of the earliest New Testament documents, this passage provides important information about the leadership structure in the early church. Luke, writing in Acts, tells us that Paul appointed elders in every church he planted (Acts 14:23). The term "elder" (*presbuteros*) reflects the language of the Jewish synagogue. In our present passage the phrases "one who is taught" and "one who teaches" both come from the Greek word *katecheo*, from which we get the English "catechumen" and "catechism."

In Paul's next letter, 1 Thessalonians, he wrote about three key functions of those who are in a role of leadership in the church. The Greek has three participles, governed by a single article, suggesting that we are looking at one group of persons who perform three tasks—labor among, have charge over, and provide instruction (5:12).

Three primary terms are used in the New Testament to describe the functions of those in leadership. The English word "elder" translates the Greek word *presbuteros*. "Pastor" translates *poimen* and "overseer" translates *episcopos*. These three terms are not titles referring to two or three different persons, but rather are descriptive of several functions of a single individual and are often used interchangeably. In Acts 20:17 we are told that Paul called on the elders of the church at Ephesus to meet him at Miletus. In verse 28 we read the charge: "Be on guard for yourselves and for all the flock, among which the Holy Spirit has made you overseers, to shepherd the church of God which He purchased with His own blood." Notice that the *elders* are called to *shepherd* and *oversee*. Similarly, Peter instructed his fellow elders, "Shepherd the flock of God among you, exercising oversight" (1 Peter 5:2).

Biblical leadership advances the Kingdom; it's not about titles. Those in such leadership positions not only deserve financial support, they deserve far more. The phrase "all good things" is sufficiently broad to mean our full participation. Paul had just taught that "each one must examine his own work" and "each one will bear his own load."

Sowing to the Spirit (6:7-8)

The opening phrase, "Do not be deceived," may be a reference to the response of some Galatians to the teaching of the Judaizers. The image of sowing and reaping is a common one and, in this context, it would certainly pick up the theme of the "fruit" of the Spirit (5:22). It is also possible that the metaphor may have come to Paul's mind because of his treatment of Christian giving in verse 6. Paul's most extensive use of the sowing and reaping metaphor is found in 2 Corinthians 9:6-15, which deals throughout with generous giving. The reminder that "God is not mocked" indicates that God knows the details of our lives and rewards our efforts.

Chapter 11

The phrase "sows to his own flesh" in verse 8 means allowing the old (lower) nature to have its own way. It means to live in such a manner that we gratify our fleshly desires. The result of such sowing will be a harvest of corruption, which corresponds to the "deeds of the flesh" mentioned in Galatians 5:19. "Corruption" refers to the moral and physical decay that accompanies such behavior in this life and becomes ultimate in the final judgment. The future tense indicates an everlasting harvest of destruction, not annihilation (cf. Dan. 12:2 and Mark 9:48).

In contrast, the person "who sows to the Spirit will . . . reap "eternal life," meaning both the present enjoyment of the life of God (John 10:10) and an eternal future in His presence where we will bear His image (1 Cor. 15:49).

Do Not Grow Weary in Doing Good (6:9-10)

Paul consistently insisted that no one can win favor with God by doing good, but he was equally as insistent that it is the Christian's duty and desire to do good. Twice in these two verses Paul repeated the phrase related to good works. Only one thing can hinder the spiritual farmer, and that is to "lose heart in doing good" (v. 9), which would cause him or her to stop the process of sowing.

The verb translated "grow weary" was sometimes used to describe becoming loose like an unstrung bow. Anyone who has been involved in Christian ministry understands what it means to feel like the unstrung bow. Human nature lacks staying power, and this is particularly true when we don't see any visible results. In Luke 18:1 Jesus warned us about losing heart when it comes to persistent prayer.

"In due time" means in God's appointed time. The Greek word *kairos*, which means "fitting season" or "opportunity," is used in both verses 9 and 10. God's timetable is perfect, and He guarantees the harvest for those who endure in sowing seed.

"While we have opportunity" (v. 10) means that we must seize every opportunity God lays before us until the day of His return. The power to persevere in good works is provided by the Holy Spirit, but the responsibility to choose to persevere is up to each believer. First, we must "do good to all people," which means that the believers' responsibility to do good must be rendered to everyone, regardless of race, nationality, class, sex, or any other artificial distinction. Nevertheless, Christians owe a special obligation to members of "the household of the faith." This phrase indicates that early Christians saw themselves as part of the same family, related by their common faith. We become family by our common faith in Christ, but we build strong family relationships by doing good to and for one another.

For Memory and Meditation

"Bear one another's burdens, and thereby fulfill the law of Christ." (Gal. 6:2)

The Freedom to Pray

"Father, help me never to be boastful or envious. Give me the strength and willingness to help shoulder the burden of others who have violated their freedom and have been caught in sin."

Chapter 12

Boast in the Cross Alone

Galatians 6:11-18

I can still remember my foolish boasting as a young child. It became a game we children played. Sometimes it involved our fathers, as in "my father can beat your father at . . ." (you fill in the blank). At other times, it focused on our own imagined abilities. I can lift more weight, run faster, jump higher, than you can. They were usually harmless games whose downside was a skinned knee or a "momentarily" wounded friendship.

Adults play a more subtle version of the boasting game. It often relates to job, income, children's achievements, social status, club memberships, leadership positions in the community or church, and the like. But, in the adult version, the outcome can be far more detrimental to our social and spiritual lives. We can buy into our own boasting and conclude that we are better than most. The boasting game can cause us to trust in our own flesh; that is, our own accomplishments.

Paul concluded this important letter to the Galatians with a few summary statements and a final, brief benediction. He indicated that persons who attempted to enforce circumcision as a necessity for salvation were doing so from improper motives. They wanted to impress their Jewish friends and relatives by demonstrating their fidelity to the Jewish traditions. They were not concerned about the spiritual progress of the new believers in Galatia; they wanted to point to them as "trophies" of their diligent work. Paul, on the other hand, would boast only in the cross.

CHAPTER 12

Writing with Large Letters (v. 11)

Writing in the first century was a difficult task, since it required time to prepare the materials necessary for the process. For that reason, it was usual for an author to utilize a professional scribe. Frequently, Paul dictated his material to a secretary known as an *amanuensis*. In some cases, the amanuensis might identify himself as we see in Romans 16:22: "I, Tertius, who write this letter, greet you in the Lord." In Colossians 4:18 Paul indicated that he had written the greeting with his own hand. In Galatians Paul penned a lengthy postscript (vv. 11-18) to call attention to the critical nature of the message.

The phrase "large letters" has been interpreted in several different ways. The translators of the King James Version interpreted it to mean the length of the letter: "Ye see how large a letter I have written unto you with mine own hand." Not only is this a short letter compared to other Pauline letters, but Paul would have used the word *epistle* if that was the meaning he intended to convey. You will discover that the New King James Version (NKJV) agrees with most other translations in using "large letters," meaning large in size.

Some commentators have said that the phrase "large letter" refers to the size of the letters, indicating that Paul's eyesight was bad. Recall that in Galatians 4:15 Paul indicated that the Galatians would have been willing to pluck their own eyes out and give them to him. If this phrase is a reference to bad eyesight, then the large sprawling letters, which had little beauty, could be a final subtle comparison of himself to those who were proud of their reputation (cf. Gal. 2:6). It is also possible that the phrase may simply mean large capital letters, rather than the smaller cursive letters. Many early manuscripts were in all capital letters and are referred to as UNCIALS. In either case, the impact of the letter is strengthened by Paul's personal appeal.

Contrasting Motives (vv. 12-14)

Throughout the letter Paul contrasted consistently the content of the authentic gospel with that put forth by the Judaizers. Here he considered the Judiazers' motives and duplicitous lifestyle. He wanted to be clear that the Judaizers were not concerned about the welfare of the Galatians; they were concerned only about their own honor. Paul pointed to three separate issues that may have guided the Judiazers' efforts to pressure the new believers in Galatia into accepting circumcision and other Jewish traditions. First, they wanted "to make a good showing in the flesh" (v. 12). Second, they wanted to avoid being "persecuted for the cross of Christ." Finally, they wanted to "boast in your flesh" (v. 13).

"A good showing in the flesh" simply means they wanted to impress their fellow Jews. We can only imagine the pressure Jews who became followers of Christ must have experienced from their Jewish family and friends. By making circumcision necessary for conversion, the Judaizers were trying to work their way back into the good graces of their relatives and former friends.

The Galatian Jewish believers must have believed that such ingratiating behavior would keep them from being persecuted by their fellow Jews. They knew full well that a Jew who departs from Jewish traditions and accepts Christ wholeheartedly can expect persecution and ostracism. In truth, their behavior toward Paul was excellent proof of the reality of their fear. The Galatians were trying to avoid Paul's fate by means of compromise. They were willing to insist that salvation is accomplished by means of faith plus law-works.

The teaching of the cross will always be opposed and will often result in persecution because it shows human sinfulness, the critical nature of Jesus's death, and the total inability of human beings to save themselves through works. For this reason, it robs the "good person" of any and every basis for human pride.

"Those who are circumcised" refers to the Jews who had been circumcised and not to the Galatians who were being pressured to accept circumcision to complete their salvation. Those who insisted on law-keeping were hypocrites because they failed to keep the whole law, and now they were trying to bind the Gentile believers to the law by insisting on the rite that was the gateway to the law.

Paul's teaching here is consistent with Jesus's condemnation of the Pharisees as hypocrites. Jesus argued that they made void the word of God by their traditions (Matt. 15:6) and, more importantly, "they tie up heavy burdens and lay them on men's shoulders, but they themselves are unwilling to move them with so much as a finger" (Matt. 23:4).

The Judaizers were motivated by the desire to win the respect of their countrymen by boasting about how many of the Galatians they persuaded to practice Jewish traditions, particularly circumcision. The word "boast" reminds us of the use of the same word in its noun form in 6:4. The only possible reason for such futile boasting would be to bolster their own cause, not to help the Galatians grow in faith.

The contrast between boasting in the "flesh" of the Galatians and boasting in "the cross of Christ" is stark and powerful. The cross is the last thing that natural humans would have ever selected as a reason for boasting. In the first century the cross was a repulsive symbol of contempt. In writing to the Corinthians, Paul called the cross a stumbling block to the Jews and foolishness to the Greeks (1 Cor. 1:23). The cross exposes man's absolute and utter spiritual bankruptcy. It reveals the folly of human pride. No one can comprehend the glory of the cross until first confronting his or her own depravity.

How do we glory in the cross? By surrendering our entire being to the crucified Christ (Gal. 2:20) and living for Him alone! We glory in it when we share it unapologetically with all persons with whom we come into contact.

Earlier Paul indicated that he had been crucified with Christ, but now he declares that "the world has been crucified to me" (v. 14). The world—including all its earthly treasures and pleasures, honors and accomplishments—has lost its appeal (cf. Phil. 3:7-11). But the statement here goes a step further as Paul declared that he was dead to the world. He was likely an object of contempt to his family and former friends. No wonder the Judaizers despised him.

What Matters Is a New Creation (vv. 15-16)

Perhaps the Judaizers would have expected Paul to boast in uncircumcision; but for him it was an empty ritual, an external marking of the body with no spiritual significance. Neither circumcision nor uncircumcision had any value toward salvation. The only thing that matters is "a new creation" (v. 15). The same idea is articulated clearly in 2 Corinthians 5:17: "Therefore if anyone is in Christ, he is a new creature; the old things passed away; behold, new things have come." The new creation is the transforming work of the Holy Spirit in the lives of those who come to the cross for redemption.

One may wonder if Paul had in mind the final words of Psalm 125:5 when he pronounced a blessing of peace upon all who "walk by this rule" (Gal. 6:16). "This rule" refers to trusting God alone for salvation through the cross of Christ. Those who follow it discover that God's mercy is available through faith in Christ, not by obedience to any religious activity on the part of humans.

Some debate exists as to the meaning of "the Israel of God." If you read this verse from several different translations, you may notice that some will translate the final phrase in verse 16 as "and upon the Israel of God," while others will translate it "even the Israel of God." The difference between "and" and "even" will determine whether one thinks Paul had in mind two different groups or a single group. The question is whether Paul used the phrase "Israel of God" to refer to all Jews; all Jews who will accept Jesus as Messiah, or all believers, be they Jew or Gentile.

The first two options seem to be counter to the entire argument of this letter. Therefore it seems likely this phrase indicates that all believers are the new Israel of God. Paul made a similar point in Philippians 3:2-3, indicating that "the true circumcision" refers to those who "worship in the Spirit of God and glory in Christ Jesus." The Judaizers wanted to offer the Galatians citizenship in Israel through circumcision. Paul affirmed that through Christ they were spiritual descendants of Abraham, "heirs according to promise" (Gal. 3:29), and therefore part of the new "Israel of God," the instrument of His purpose.

The Brand-Marks of Jesus (v. 17)

Both the Judaizers and the Galatians who had been influenced by them had caused trouble for Paul. The word translated "trouble" is used by Paul in other contexts for the toil that is characteristic of the ministry of a true shepherd; but in this context it has a negative connotation. Those who cause trouble require attention and energy that is exhausting and deprive other persons or communities of the care they may legitimately need. We often forget that our spiritual leaders do not have endless time and energy; and therefore when we consume either unwisely, we are depriving someone else whose needs may be greater than our own.

Many commentators believe that "brand-marks of Jesus" refers to the physical marks left on Paul's body by the persecution he encountered while traveling through Galatia during his first missionary journey. At Pisidian Antioch, after Paul announced his strategy of preaching to the Gentiles, the Jews instigated a persecution against Paul and Barnabas and drove them out of town (Acts 13:50). At Lystra, Jews stoned Paul, dragged him out of the city, and left him for dead (Acts 14:19). The scars proved that Paul was Christ's servant.

Likely the reference in Galatians 6:17 to the marks of Jesus in Paul's flesh is an ironic contrast to the meaningless marks of circumcision so valued by the Judaizers. His opponents were not to trouble him further, for his marks indicated he was Jesus's man. The logical conclusion is that anyone who troubled Paul was grieving his Savior.

Final Benediction (v. 18)

Paul normally concluded his letters with a benediction that indicates his desire for the recipients to know God's grace (cf. 2 Cor. 13:14; Eph. 6:24; Phil. 4:27; Col. 4:18). Some persons have suggested that the brevity of this benediction is related to the tension that is expressed throughout the letter. That seems unlikely, since Paul used the intimate term "brethren."

Despite the brevity of the benediction, it has both beauty and profundity. The focus on grace is a meaningful contrast with the works required by the Judaizers. Grace is "with [their] spirit," meaning their inner being, as contrasted with meaningless marks on the outer flesh. Paul used the full title "Lord Jesus Christ." "Lord" means that He owns and guards us, and as willing servants we should do His bidding. As Jesus, He alone is Savior. As the Christ (Messiah), He alone is qualified to be our Prophet, High Priest, and eternal King.

For Memory and Meditation

"But may it never be that I would boast, except in the cross of our Lord Jesus Christ, through which the world has been crucified to me, and I to the world." (Gal. 6:14)

The Freedom to Pray

"Father, keep me from prideful boasting. Today I will boast only in the cross of the Lord Jesus, who by His death set me free. Help me to live for You daily."

Epilogue

Johnny Hunt

I can still remember the night my father chose to leave our family. I was seven years old; by no means did I fully understand everything about the fact my mother and father were divorcing. However, as a result, I was raised along with my five siblings by a single mom. My mother worked in a factory during the day and as a restaurant server at night to provide for six children. We ended up in a government project in Wilmington, North Carolina. I stayed in and out of trouble as a teenage boy and at the age of sixteen made the terrible decision to drop out of high school. I spent a good bit of my days hanging out at the poolroom in Sunset Park and began to work there as well as attempt to hustle pool. My passionate desire at the time was to be able to play pool professionally. However, when I was twenty years old, a man by the name of N. W. Pridgen invited my wife, Janet, and me to church. Janet had been encouraging me to go to church at the pressing of her godly grandmother. I put her off as long as I could. Finally, when I decided to go, we went to Long Leaf Baptist Church where Mr. Pridgen attended.

After hearing the gospel for a couple of weeks, the Holy Spirit used God's Word to bring me under conviction. When I use the word *conviction*, I am simply referring to how the Holy Spirit used the good news of Jesus to display and expose my need for a Savior. I did not really know what all of that meant, but God was certainly touching my heart. At the close of a morning service, the pastor said that he sensed a young man was being dealt with by God, and he asked the congregation to join him in praying that the young man would come back that night and be saved. I knew

Epilogue

that he was referring to me; God was undoubtedly calling me by name. Sometimes people ask me if I felt that God really had my number. I am grateful to know that He is far more personal than that; He calls us by name. That afternoon, instead of desiring to go to Hollywood Drag Strip to race and watch the races, we went to church. I had never been in a Sunday school class, never attended a revival, and never owned a Bible. However, the call of God upon my heart was more than I could resist. When the pastor asked people to respond to Jesus, I hesitated because I was so shy. I finally slipped out of my seat. As I went forward, I gave my hand to Mr. M. E. Gibson and my heart to the Lord Jesus Christ.

Charles Haddon Spurgeon, a famous British pastor, often said that when he was converted he lost 80 percent of his vocabulary. I can call God as my witness that the Lord changed my vocabulary. He literally changed my "want to's." God did something deep within my heart that Romans 12:2 refers to as a transformation. He literally transformed my heart, my mind, and my life on that Sunday evening at Long Leaf Baptist Church. I have had my ups and downs, but God has remained more faithful and steady than any friend I have ever known. I know what it means to be "free indeed."

Romans 10:13 is a precious promise and such a simple truth: "Whoever will call on the name of the Lord will be saved." I am so glad that I asked the Lord Jesus to forgive me of my sins, come into my life, and give me true freedom. My friend, it would bring me great joy if *you* would invite Him today to be *your* Savior. Let me explain as concisely, clearly, and compellingly as I can what it means to be saved.

1. The Bible teaches that when a person is saved, Jesus cleanses that person of his or her sins. All of them! Colossians 2:14 teaches that He takes our sins out of the way by nailing them to the cross.

Christ died on the cross, paying the penalty for sin. He died in your place so that you can experience His abundant and eternal life.

2. As a young man, I struggled when I thought about trusting Christ, whether I would be able to live out the Christian life. I realized that living it out wasn't up to me. The Lord promises, in the person of the Holy Spirit, to come into your life. He will produce the fruit of His life in and through yours. He will never leave you, never forsake you. It really is an exchange: I give Him my life; He gives me His. Galatians 2:20 puts it this way: "I have been crucified with Christ; and it is no longer I who live, but Christ lives in me; and the life which I now live in the flesh I live by faith in the Son of God, who loved me and gave Himself up for me."

3. As if forgiveness of sin and God living in me through the Holy Spirit were not enough, He has given me everlasting life. Each of us will face death. I have the eternal hope that to be absent from the body is to be present with the Lord (2 Cor. 5:8). I have a home in heaven that Jesus has prepared for me and for those who put their trust in Him as Lord and Savior.

If you have not done so, experience what this book talks about—true freedom in Christ. By His grace we are free to live as we ought to live! God offers this to us through His Son, the Lord Jesus. Trust Him today by simply praying this prayer:

> Lord Jesus, I need You. I know that I cannot save myself. Come into my life and forgive me of my sins. Take up residence in me and live Your life through me. Thank You today for hearing my prayer and giving me the gift of eternal life. Please help me to never be ashamed of You. In Jesus's name, amen.

If you made that prayer yours, I pray that you will contact us at ken@auxanopress.com. We want the opportunity to rejoice and welcome you to God's forever family.

Auxano Press Non-Disposable Curriculum

- Designed for use in any small group
- Affordable, biblically based, and life oriented
- Choose your own material and stop and start times
- Study the Bible and build a Christian library

For teaching guides and additional small group study materials, or to learn about other Auxano Press titles, visit Auxanopress.com.

Other Books by Ken Hemphill

In 1 Corinthians Paul anchors the Christian life in the grace of God, affirming that our eyes, ears, and hearts have not yet comprehended all God has prepared. If you want to know what God has in store for you and your church, study *Living from Grace to Glory* and discover what you have to offer Christ through His church.

The Letters of Paul provides an intimate glimpse into the apostle Paul's life through the lens of his personal letters to churches and church leaders. You will sense Paul's love for Christ and His church as you follow Paul's missionary journeys. Each chapter, in chronological order, places one of Paul's letters in its original historical context and discusses why the Spirit prompted the great Apostle to the Gentiles to write the letter.

Some of the greatest texts and most encouraging promises in all of Scripture are found in Paul's second letter to the Corinthians. Paul's integrity was being attacked, and his altered travel plans fortified some of his detractors in their accusations. Paul's response to the attacks levied against him will not only give you an intimate portrait of the great apostle, you will also discover clear directions for effective ministry in a fallen world and an imperfect church.

For teaching guides and additional small group study materials, or to learn about other Auxano Press titles, visit **Auxanopress.com**.

Jesus sent the Holy Spirit to make the church His main priority. The day of Pentecost was just the beginning; the Holy Spirit wants to empower, enliven, encourage, mobilize, pray, teach, equip, and protect our churches now!

The eight chapters in *Empowered: Why We Need Spirit-Filled Churches* introduce you to the Spirit's powerful, practical ministries in the local church today. The church is utterly dependent upon the Spirit and is doomed without Him. In this fast-paced book you will be reminded the Holy Spirit is the presence and power of God for our churches right here and right now.

For teaching guides and additional small group study materials, or to learn about other Auxano Press titles, visit **Auxanopress.com.**